RICE & PEAS AND FISH & CHIPS

ONE WOMAN'S STORY
OF OVERCOMING RACISM

RICE & PEAS AND FISH & CHIPS

ONE WOMAN'S STORY
OF OVERCOMING RACISM

PAULINE CAMPBELL

TWENTY SEVEN

First edition published in 2021 by Imprint Twenty Seven,
an imprint of Nobrow Ltd. 27 Westgate Street, London, E8 3RL

Rice & Peas and Fish &Chips
© Pauline Campbell, 2021

Printed and bound by Ozgraf in Poland
on FSC® certified paper

Cover art © Daniel Clarke, 2021

Graphic design by Justin Moore

FSC
www.fsc.org

MIX
Paper from
responsible sources
FSC® C163799

ISBN: 978-1-914343-01-8

www.imprint27.com
www.nobrow.net

To Dad and Mum

CONTENTS

FOREWORD
BY COLIN FREEMAN

People reading this book may think I'm the last person who should be writing the foreword. And to some extent, I'd agree. For a start, I'm white, not Black. I grew up in a village in Scotland in the 1970s, not an inner-city suburb of London or Manchester. I've spent much of my life working as a journalist for *The Daily Telegraph* – not generally the paper of choice among the Black residents of Hackney or Moss Side. My main work is as a foreign correspondent, writing about far-off elections and distant wars. Anything, in other words, but modern, multi-cultural Britain.

Like many hacks, though, I do dream of being a columnist, and in 2015 I chanced to write a *Telegraph* blog about the death of the actor Terry Sue-Patt. To millions of 70s children, Sue-Patt was better known as Benny Green from *Grange Hill*, the BBC TV drama about life in a London comprehensive school. Benny was one of the show's best-loved characters, and to kids like me, from Britain's all-white provinces, he was also our first introduction to a Black child our own age. No, he didn't look like us, but he certainly seemed like us: a cheerful lad who enjoyed a laugh, and stuck up for his mates.

My argument in the blog was that Benny, perhaps, did as much for integration in Britain as any well-intended race relations teaching. And right or wrong, my blog certainly got a lot of traffic.

Then, out of the blue earlier this year, Pauline Campbell got in touch. The piece had struck a chord with her, she said, and she was planning to mention it in her book, *Rice & Peas and Fish & Chips*. Not only that, would I be willing to write the book's foreword? Flattered as I was, I did ask her whether a white fellow from the sticks was really the right choice. She said that was precisely the point. She wanted to reach out to a wider audience – a bit like Benny Green did all those years ago.

Reading Pauline's accounts of growing up in Hackney and Tottenham, I'm reminded that for all *Grange Hill* might have said that all kids were the same, things were more complicated than that. I've never suffered racism, or the feeling of not quite fitting in. It's profoundly sad to read of her looking at herself in the mirror as a youngster and wishing she wasn't Black, and of how that knocked her off course just when she could have been doing well at school. And all the more impressive that Pauline never gave up, not only qualifying as a lawyer, but also pursuing her writing career.

No, I don't agree with everything that Pauline writes, (*What did you expect from a* Telegraph *hack, Pauline...?)* But this book is a touching, heartfelt insight into a world very different to my own, where to this day, life chances simply aren't equal from the day we're born.

I'm no expert in sociology or race relations, but on that subject of equality, let me finish with a little anecdote of my own. In her opening pages, Pauline writes about wrapping up her late father's affairs in the probate office in Holborn, looking around at the other Black families in the waiting room, and wondering what their lives had been like.

It reminded me of a day back in 2010, when my first child was born. In a waiting room at the maternity ward were me and a Black dad to be. We didn't talk much, beyond briefly wishing each other luck. But I sometimes wonder what happened to his son, born at the same time and place as my daughter, yet quite possibly with very different life prospects. Hopefully, one day those life prospects will be exactly the same.

Waldes Campbell, 1937–2013

A EULOGY

On Saturday 21 September, 2013, a bright early autumn morning, I stood at the doorway of the family room of North Middlesex Hospital, London. My elder sister, Joyce, and my mother, Gwen, beckoned me in.

I refused.

The open doorway revealed a small room filled with clutter, shelves stacked with books and magazines; a pair of blue overalls hung over the back of a chair. Through the glass panels to the adjoining room sat two nurses, but I couldn't say what they were doing. For all I knew they could have been working, or on their break, eating, drinking or chatting.

'Pauline, you need to come in,' Joyce said.

'No,' I replied, still resolute. 'No.'

I'd got the call at six o'clock that morning – Joyce, her voice strained and urgent, summoning me to the hospital, 'You need to come . . . now,' she'd said – and I *knew*.

I'd managed the drive there, my knuckles tight on the steering wheel, heart pounding in my throat; made the long, lonely walk through the whitewashed corridors, seen the look on my sister and mum's faces that made it clear what they were about to say. *I didn't want to hear it*. My feet were glued to the ground; I couldn't move.

Adamant, my sister let out a sigh and came over to me. She took my hands in hers, looked me in the eye and said, 'He's gone.'

My throat tightened and panic clawed my stomach, as if wrenching out my insides. I screamed, fell to the floor outside that family room and cried, 'No! Daddy!' It was like something had hit me with a ferocity that knocked me off my feet. The feeling of loss was crippling. 'No, no, Daddy, Daddy!' It didn't matter that I was in my forties – a grown woman. At that moment I felt like a child again, a child who had lost something so precious it could never be replaced.

My sister pulled me to my feet and ushered me into the room where Mum was waiting. The three of us sat down, Joyce on one side, I on the other. We both gripped Mum's hands as she rocked back and forth.

'Lard God,' she wailed, 'Campbell's gone, Campbell's gone.'

Shortly after, my younger brothers, Fitz and Glen, arrived with my older sister, Anne.

'What's happened? What is it?' they all asked at once, their faces pinched and drawn. As the awful news hit them we merged together in grief, consoling one another, *consoling Mum*.

A nurse entered the room and said softly, 'He's ready for you to say goodbye.'

I wasn't sure I wanted to go. I didn't want to remember Daddy like that. But Mum got up, and my brothers, sisters and I instinctively followed. The walk towards St Mary's ward was frightening because I knew what was at the end of it. I took a deep breath and clung on to Mum's arm.

We entered the ward. The nurse pulled back the curtain round the bed and there he was. *Dad*. Waldes Campbell, quiet, no longer in pain and at peace; by his side the small radio I had bought for him, still tuned in to his favourite reggae station.

My heartache intensified as I agonised about not kissing him the evening before. I'd tried, but it was awkward as he lay in the hospital bed. Joyce had made more of an effort, manoeuvring herself over him and planting a wet, sticky kiss on his cheeks.

'That's how you do it,' she said as we said our goodbyes, telling him we would see him the following day.

We all stood around the bed in which he lay, with the morning sun streaming through the window. My sisters touched his face and kissed his hands. I can't remember if I kissed him. *I hope I did.*

I loved Dad, but there was a distance between us, one that didn't exist between him and my sisters. Dad's favourite line was that he had five children, and when he told them to do something four of them would say, 'Yes, Daddy', but I would always say, 'Why, Daddy?' Mum said we were cut from the same cloth, meaning we were too alike – strong-willed to the point of stubbornness. But he was my dad, and no matter how difficult things were between us, *I loved him.*

Waldes Campbell was born in the Parish of St Elizabeth, Jamaica, on 21 May, 1937, second child to Ivy and Beres Campbell. Dad lost his mother at the age of four. One day she was there and the next she was gone, he told us. Dad grew up with his grandparents and other relatives after being deserted by his father who went to America and never looked back.

As I gazed at his lifeless body, I had no idea what to say. Dad was the lynchpin, the foundation on which our lives had been built. He grew up without much love, but he made sure we knew the security of a loving family.

Alongside the enormous sadness came the words from Mum as she held Dad's hand and said her goodbyes. 'Campbell, I want to tank you for sending fe me, for bringing me to England. I know how hard it was for you, and dat yu could have made a new life here without me, but you chose to send fe me and give me and your family the chance of a better life. Tank you. . . '

Parts of that day are imprinted within me, whilst others are impossible to recollect, but I'll never forget how hard it was leaving the hospital carrying two plastic bags containing Dad's personal effects.

As the solicitor of the family, I was allotted the task of dealing with the bureaucracy of Dad's passing, sorting out the mounds of paperwork involved in probate. Dad was a private man who, like most West Indians, guarded his personal affairs fiercely, so it was a little unnerving going through his bank accounts, insurance policies and pensions. I half-expected him to come in and lambast me for *interfering in his business*.

It was a difficult time for all of us. Funerals can do one of two things – they can either bond a family or tear it apart. I am glad to say that, although at times we had the odd disagreement regarding the arrangements, we stayed strong as a family unit, with Mum at the helm keeping us focused and together. But every so often, you'd find one of us crying in a corner, dealing with the loss in our own way, as we ensured we surrounded Mum with the badly needed love of her children. Although we cried, we also found time to laugh about our Waldes Campbell, as other family and friends came to the house to support us armed with chicken, fried fish, hard dough bread and strong drinks including a lot of white Jamaican rum.

My brother Fitz loved rice. Whenever Mum cooked it, his plate of food would never be enough, so Fitz was known for scraping the bottom of the rice pot until it was clean. It was a running joke that even the burnt bits of rice weren't spared.

One day, Fitz was playing up and got on the bad side of Dad, who just looked at him and said, 'Bwoy, what is wrong wid yu, mussy the burnt-up rice gone to yu head.' Dad didn't even realise it was funny, but we were all cracking up. There are countless stories like that, and we must have gone through them all that day.

On 24 December, 2013, the probate office finalised Dad's Estate. I checked the sealed document, accepting the finality of it all. As I sat in that office on Holborn Road among other Caribbean children who had also lost a loved one, it dawned on me that we were all there for the same reason, but we didn't talk to each other, stuck in our own little pockets of grief.

The scariest part of all was that it reflected how I had lived my life. Of course, I had my family and friends, but as I looked around the room and identified with other Black people, I was filled with sorrow because, although our parents and the generation that followed would have had similar experiences, I felt as though we as a race had become fragmented.

I wanted to discover more about their backgrounds. I wished I had the courage to pull up a chair and sit beside them, ask them about their dads or mums: find out when they'd arrived, what their life had been like in Britain. But I didn't dare take the journey across the length of that open room, and that night as I lay in bed and looked out at the silent night sky, I felt an overwhelming sense of guilt as I realised why. It was safer not to. I had to maintain that cloak of security, the one telling me that I'd had to fight too hard to become a solicitor to concern myself with what had happened and what *was happening* to those in my community.

It became apparent that everything I had achieved, the adversity I had overcome, was because of an inner strength, one I would not have had, but for the courage of my dad and mum. After achieving my goals I put all my efforts into maintaining my place, because those of us born enclosed in a Black skin have to work twice as hard to prove ourselves in the professional world in which we work. But the pitfall was that, somewhere in that world, I had forgotten where I was coming from.

Renowned civil rights activist and author Maya Angelou said, 'You can't really know where you are going until you know where you have been.'[1]

I wanted to take that journey, find out 'where I had been'. At first, I questioned whether I would be committed enough to see this gargantuan project through. But that was just an excuse, because my real concern was the doubt I had in myself – not in my ability, but in my qualification to pen such a piece. Strangely, I wasn't sure if I was *Black enough*.

Although I know I originate from Africa, I cannot deny that a chasm exists between my West Indian and African ancestry. I find myself detached from my African ancestral past, which, if anything, only emphasises my Britishness. Whilst I may see myself as British, there are some who would oppose that view.

In 1968, Conservative MP Enoch Powell stated, 'The West Indian or Asian does not, by being born in England, become an Englishman. In law he becomes a United Kingdom citizen by birth; in fact, he is a West Indian or Asian still.'[2]

But what can be defined as a true Englishman? It is thought that the first modern Britons, who lived about 10,000 years ago, had 'dark to black' skin, according to a ground-breaking DNA analysis of Britain's oldest complete skeleton. The fossil, known as Cheddar Man, was unearthed more than a century ago at Gough's Cave in Somerset. Intense speculation has built up around Cheddar Man's origins and appearance because he lived shortly after the first settlers crossed from continental Europe to Britain at the end of the last Ice Age. People of white British ancestry alive today are said to be descendants of this population.[3]

Whether you agree with the scientists or not, this is more than just a question of who was in Britain first. It goes a lot deeper than that. My upbringing encompasses language, religious beliefs, education, social interaction and so much more. Surely that must play a part in being considered part of British society? I do not agree with Powell that my Britishness is diminished in some way merely because of my West Indian origins. For the past fifty-plus years, I have immersed myself in British society. I am a product of everything my generation stood for when our parents decided to make a life for themselves in Britain. I did not have a choice in that, but, like most of my generation, I chose to embrace the society in which I lived because *it was the only home I knew*.

On the day I lost my father I became a member of an exclusive club, a club none of us wanted to join: a generation – *my generation*

– born in 1960s Britain, brought up on both rice and peas and fish and chips, whose parents crossed thousands of miles, leaving the warm shores of the Caribbean to settle in Britain. If I was cast on to a desert island for the rest of my life and given the option of one dish to take with me, I would find it almost impossible to choose between rice and peas and fish and chips. Would selecting one over the other make me more or less British in the eyes of my peers and society in general?

In writing this book I am taking a journey into *where* my generation and *I have been*, a journey that began with Dad and so many like him when they came to Britain. I will reveal what I, and those of my generation, faced as we were described as 'wide-grinning piccaninnies', 'educationally subnormal' and the 'Alien Wedge'. To my parents, I represented the *expectation of change, a better life*, filled with hope and opportunities they'd never had. But neither they nor I had any idea that subsequent events would lead to a tsunami of inequality that would have a ripple effect on not just me and those of us who were the first generation of children born to our parents on British shores, but also on the generation that followed. We were to become key players, pawns, in a game of chess, in which we were used – beginning in the post-war years and spanning over five decades – to secure votes for Labour, the Conservatives and extreme right-wing groups. In unravelling the threads of this racism, I will show what enables it to flourish and, most importantly, what makes its beneficiaries so resistant to change.

THE LEGACY OF NOTTING HILL

CHAPTER
I

In the words of Chinese philosopher Laozi, 'The journey of a thousand miles begins with one step.'[4] However, the difficulty I faced was that I was not sure what that first step would be. I assumed it would be the year 1961, when Dad arrived in Britain, but the significance of events that took place three years before would send shock waves through the West Indian community and shape Dad's and my generation's lives for decades to come.

Every area of London comes with its own history, and there is one part of West London where this is no exception. Today you can enjoy a tour of Notting Hill, pose by the blue door or go into the bookshop from the 1999 film *Notting Hill*, starring Hugh Grant and Julia Roberts, see where the area's most famous residents lived and visit the restaurants and bars of this trendy urban village. You can take in the buzz of the world-famous Portobello Road Market, see buskers, visit spice shops and cafés, and taste delicious international dishes prepared at the market stalls.

In my younger days, I would excitedly get myself ready and meet with friends to make the yearly jaunt to the Notting Hill Carnival during the August bank holiday. Carnival was like a melting pot; people from all over the world would come to experience it, and – the best part – you could dance in the street in an atmosphere where you could put any differences between cultures aside. Carnival floats and costumes created a living colourful collage.

It was only recently, though, that I became aware of how –
and, more importantly, why – the Notting Hill Carnival came
into being. The fashionable Notting Hill we see today, with its
houses and flats often valued in excess of a million pounds,
could not be more different to the area known for the slum
housing that existed in the West London borough just fifty
years before.

After the Second World War, parts of Britain were in ruins;
the rebuilding of cities required a number of labourers, more
than Britain had at its disposal. Originally, soldiers were req-
uisitioned for the task, and prisoners of war were also used.
But the numbers proved insufficient, and the government had
to seek help further afield.

On 22 June, 1948, the *Empire Windrush*, shadowed by an
English warship as it entered the British Channel, docked
from Jamaica, carrying 492 Caribbean passengers. That same
year, the Labour government passed the British Nationality Act,
which granted United Kingdom citizenship to all people from
the then-current and former British colonies. British passports were issued and the right to come and live in Britain was
granted for life. Dad had no idea at the time, living in Jamaica
at just eleven years old, that this significant piece of legislation
was the catalyst that would change his life.

Many West Indians settled in Notting Hill because the rents
were low and they were able to find accommodation in 'houses
of multiple occupancy', an opportunity that had to be grasped
given the various colour bars in place. At the time, Notting Hill
was made up of two areas – Colville, full of run-down tene-
ment houses populated by the West Indian community, and
slum-ridden Notting Dale, which had a large, close-knit, white
working-class population. A working-class white community
who found it virtually impossible to borrow money to improve
their living standards, and faced with harsher rationing and
a shortage of decent housing, had little empathy for their

West Indian neighbours, interpreting the Black migrants, forced overcrowding as a cultural lifestyle decision.[5]

In the Notting Hill of the 1950s, Teddy boys were prevalent figures, identified by their drape jackets, drainpipe trousers, and crepe-soled shoes, or brothel-creepers. They were also recognisable by their hair, slicked back in a quiff commonly referred to as 'the DA'. This subculture of 'Teds' was made up of white working-class youth, discontented and disenchanted with life in post-war Britain. The National Service Act of 1948 had conscripted able-bodied men between the ages of eighteen and thirty into the armed forces for eighteen months, and this was increased to two years in 1950 in response to the British involvement in the Korean War, which was more onerous than elsewhere in Europe.[6]

Teddy boys of the 1950s were notorious for their use of flick knifes and switchblades,[7] and, to a Conservative Britain, these young people were seen as undisciplined and deviant. They were regularly banned from dances and generally unwelcome within society.[8] The treatment of the Teddy boys shows how common themes of negative perception can result in labels being placed on a group purely because they are seen as being different; a 1955 headline in the *Sunday Dispatch* stated: DANCE HALLS, CINEMAS, POLICE AND PUBLIC JOIN FORCES TO WAGE WAR ON TEDDY BOYS. As one Ted told a reporter in the accompanying article, 'We get barred from a lot of dances, they see our gear and say they don't want you in 'ere.'[9] Skinheads, mods, rockers, punks – all predominantly white youths – were also ostracised by society in subsequent years, illustrating how little things would change.

But in the 1950s this lack of belonging made these young Teds prime fodder for the likes of Oswald Mosley's Union Movement and Colin Jordan's White Defence League. Far-right political groups, angry at the numbers of West Indians entering Britain, called for curbs on immigration and the repatriation of migrants living in Britain, as well as labelling Black people as criminals and sexually deviant. With offices in Notting Hill, racist organisations such as these would hand out leaflets with slogans urging 'Keep Britain White', targeting a white community where there was already some degree of racial tension. This tension was exacerbated in 1956 by an active recruitment drive for industrial labour, with London Transport sending several representatives to Barbados, offering not just careers, but loans to pay passage to England.[10] On the one hand, you had right-wing groups calling for immigration controls, and on the other, active recruitment drives were being conducted throughout the West Indies, encouraging people to come to Britain. How many West Indians would have answered that call had they known what was lying in wait for them there?

Leading up to the August bank holiday of 1958 there had been a series of small incidents in Notting Hill, but the violence really began in late August, 1958, when a group of nine white teenagers assembled, loaded a boot of a car with metal bars, hammers and other implements, then drove around Notting Hill over a period of four hours and set upon any Black person they could find on their own or in the company of one other person, at most.

But despite the perpetrators being tracked down by the police the following day, on the hot bank holiday of 30 August, 1958, a week later, racist Teddy boys led hundreds of white people in an assault on the West Indian community. Homes of Black people were vandalised, while threatening crowds gathered and roamed the streets. Eyewitness accounts tell of several hundred people, all white, shouting obscene remarks like, 'We'll get the Black bastards.'[11]

This sustained attack on West Indians continued for days, with Black people opting to stay indoors, too terrified to go out. But on the evening of 2 September, amidst a lack of protection from the police, the Black community decided enough was enough.

A meeting was organised in the Blues Club at 9 Blenheim Crescent and the Black community made preparations for retaliation. Black resident Baron Baker saw a huge gathering of white people on Kensington Park Road and the Portobello Road. He heard someone shout, 'Let's burn the niggers, let's lynch the niggers,' at which point the Black community threw a Molotov cocktail out of the window.[12] It was only after convoys of Jamaicans from Brixton came to help defend the residents that the police brought in reinforcements from all over London to cope with the disturbances. One hundred and forty people were arrested, the majority of them white youths, although a number of Black people carrying offensive weapons were also arrested. Ultimately, 108 people were charged with crimes, including grievous bodily harm, relating to the riots, which continued until Tuesday 5 September when police finally regained control.

The newspapers and the country at large were in no doubt that the unrest in Notting Hill was racially motivated. However, despite the evidence before them and the provision of witness statements, the police's report to the Home Office stated:

These events were much publicised in the national press as race riots. Whereas there was some ill feeling between white and coloured residents in this area, it is abundantly clear much of the damage was caused by ruffians, both coloured and white, who seized the opportunity to indulge in hooliganism.[13]

Chief Superintendent Merricks was in charge of Race Relations, and when asked whether he accepted that there was racial discrimination within the police he stated: 'I think it's fair to say that we [the police] are a cross-section of society and therefore, inevitably, there will be prejudice amongst our members. But I think the important thing is whether we allow this prejudice to influence us in the way we carry out our duties.'[14]

Is it really ever possible for a police officer *not* to allow their prejudices to influence the way in which they carry out their duties? I don't believe that it is, particularly as statements given to journalist Ed Pilkington by retired police officers who had been on duty during the 1958 riots maintained, 'The reason they arrest Black people is because they are committing all the crime, and you don't pick up the white people because they don't commit crime.'[15] It is startling that Merricks made no reference to any intentions of the police to address the prejudices within the force, which instead appeared to be an accepted by-product.

The reluctance of the police to accept the mistreatment of the Black community was accompanied by a lack of recognition of their treatment within the political establishment. North Kensington MP George Rogers told the government they were at fault for failing to introduce legislation to deal with the *racial problem*, and local London MPs Henry Hynd, Frank Tomney and Albert Evans brought forward a cross-party motion in Parliament that pressed for immigration restrictions.[16]

These politicians helped to perpetuate the racial disharmony, even arguing that the Black community was responsible for high crime rates and housing shortages. Equally perplexing, the British people who accepted the opinions of MPs like Rogers seemed to have developed a form of amnesia, as if they too deliberately chose to forget that these problems were in existence long before the West Indian community arrived on British shores. Parliament statistics reveal crime rates in the UK had quadrupled from 250 crimes per 100,000 people in 1901 to 1,000 crimes per 1,000 people by 1950.[17]

It would be easy for me to step back from the events of 1958. I wasn't even born, so why should I allow the riots to affect me? Nonetheless, they do, because they had a profound effect on those who came before me and paved the way for Dad, as well as the rest of my family. It is abundantly clear that the ill will towards the Black community continued to gain momentum – a momentum that would ultimately lead to the first known racially motivated murder of someone within the Black community.

On 17 May, 1959, just eight months after the Notting Hill riots, thirty-two-year-old Antiguan carpenter Kelso Cochrane was walking home from hospital, his arm in a sling, when he was attacked by three Teddy boys. Two ambushed him from behind whilst the third stabbed him fatally in the chest. Eyewitnesses said they heard repeated racist abuse directed at Cochrane, but the police insisted the crime was not racially motivated. It was hard to watch the black-and-white footage of Kelso's coffin being carried into the church at Ladbroke Grove and to accept the fact that no one in the community who witnessed the murder came forward. A number of mourners were angry, blaming right-wing extremists, and, although they played a key role in stirring up hatred borne of mistrust of the Black community, it was impossible to ignore those who were equally complicit in stirring up the tensions that led to this act of violence that ended a man's life. Those sitting in Parliament calling for tighter immigration controls, describing Black people as 'a problem', gave legitimacy to the hate.

Decades later, as I danced in the streets at the Notting Hill Carnival, I was oblivious to the fact that this celebration of West Indian culture, first held in 1959 in St Pancras Town Hall, was created as a way of healing the fractured community and bringing it together with the white residents following the death of Kelso Cochrane.

The Carnival was the brainchild of Trinidadian-American activist Claudia Jones, who came to Britain in 1955 after being deported from America for being a member of the Communist Party.

When Claudia arrived, she was confronted with the discriminatory restrictions faced by Black people – colour bars, lack of opportunity, systemic racism. Claudia fought against.

the prejudice. She wrote poetry, attended drama school and combined all her creative talents with her journalistic skills to found the *West Indian Gazette*, the first newspaper for West Indians living in Britain. Completely self-funded, it provided information about Britain as well as the West Indies.

Claudia also recognised the difficulties Black women faced in how they were perceived. Since the era of slavery, their beauty had been suppressed. Marika Sherwood, Claudia's friend and biographer, author of *Claudia Jones: A Life in Exile* revealed that Claudia had once said, with tears in her eyes, 'We were told that we simply could not be beautiful.'[18] Claudia began to hold beauty competitions to show that Black women were just as beautiful as white women. They resulted in Black women securing jobs as models as well as in the theatre. There is no doubt that much controversy surrounds beauty competitions, and it may seem perplexing that Claudia, with her political ideals, would support the celebration of beauty in this way. But that's what made her unique: she saw it as a means, not only of boosting the confidence of Black women, but also of opening the doors of opportunity.

As a dark-skinned Black woman, I don't see many people like me in the world of British film and fashion. The first dark-skinned British model that became an icon to me was Naomi Campbell, who alongside fellow supermodel Iman in 2013, supported the Balance Diversity campaign, launched by model agent Bethann Hardison to stamp out racism and discrimination in the fashion world. Together they formed 'The Diversity Coalition'. In an interview given to Channel 4 News, Naomi highlighted that in New York Fashion Week in 2013 the percentage of Black models working was only 6 per cent and the percentage of Asian models was 9 per cent. Naomi experienced racism, it motivated her and gave her more drive to pursue her career.[19]

People like Claudia Jones started the process of creating opportunities for Black women within the British beauty industry, but it's frustrating how difficult it still is after all this time for women of colour to gain entry. Vanessa Walters, novelist, and playwright, provides an apt description of this amazing woman stating, 'What Claudia has done through the Carnival is establish West Indian culture at the heart of British society.'[20]

The legacy of the Notting Hill riots cannot be understated. The police's denial that Kelso Cochrane's murder was racially motivated, and that prejudice sparked the previous summer's riots, was a defining moment in post-war British history and would sully relations between the Black community and the Metropolitan Police for decades to follow.[21]

DAD
ARRIVES

CHAPTER II

Waldes and Gwen Campbell's wedding day, January 1963

Dad was just twenty-four when he arrived in Britain. He'd left behind a successful business in Jamaica selling vegetables and flowers to restaurants and hotels, and hoped to use his business acumen to make a better life in the UK. But his dreams of picking up where he'd left off were short-lived. There were jobs, but the opportunities were limited to industrial labour, despite the fact that 87 per cent of men and 95 per cent of women who came to Britain from the Caribbean were skilled workers.[22]

Many young men and women were employed in occupations for which they were over-qualified. Dad went from running his own business to becoming a porter at the London Underground station, Willesden Green, working early and late shifts, cleaning up and carrying out general labour. He was one of many West Indians whose potential was constrained by the limited employment options. As I was growing up, Dad would always say to me, 'No matter what, never let others stop yu from being all yu can be, because they will try to stop yu, break yu down.' Although I listened, I never really heard or understood until later in my life, especially after Dad had passed. It was only then that I was able to look at his life, *his disappointment*.

Waldes Campbell was the strongest man I ever knew, but with that strength came a resentment of the way he was treated in Britain – something he never got over. Mum told me that before I was born, and just after he had secured a job on a building site, there was a truck that had to be moved. Dad did not think twice about jumping into the vehicle and taking the wheel. But as he was about to move off, a white workman came over to him and said, 'What you doing in there? Get out, that's not your job!' Dad had confided to Mum that he'd felt humiliated and angry.

What could Dad have become had he been given the same options as his white counterparts? It hurt to consider the devastating effect this lack of opportunity had on Dad's life. Because he was such a fighter, he never accepted the inequality. There was so much more to him. Growing up, I did not understand his pain and anger, which makes me feel awful now he's gone. It's heartbreaking that I never got the chance to sit down with him, *talk to him*, about what he went through.

Why didn't he just go back to Jamaica? Because of *me*, Mum and my sisters and brothers. Dad, like most West Indian fathers, never said much about his feelings, but reading these words from a Caribbean migrant has helped to provide me with some understanding:

These have been the hardest years of my life. I think about them, and I ask myself, Sonny, tell the truth, coming here, was it a good decision or not? Think before you answer, like your dead mother used to say. So I think. And I answer, 'Yes,' it was good that we came and that we stayed. I found work; my wife is happy, happy enough. My children are happy and healthy. I thank the good Lord for all of that. I thank Him every day, just as my dead mother told me I should. I pray to Him and I ask Him. I wish too. I wish this could be like this and that could be like that. I wish I were with my family, my father, my brother, my cousins. I wish I lived in a newer home, and made more money, I wish I could have come here and be treated like I was equal by all these people. But I came as someone they thought was a dope smuggler, and that's about the way they treat me. . . [23]

MY
LIFE
BEGINS

CHAPTER III

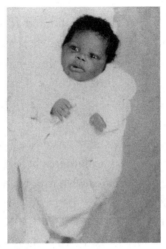

Pauline born in June 1964

Hope would become an apt description of 1964, the year of my birth. The Beatles took the world by a storm as they travelled to America for the first time and were met by hordes of screaming fans. Cassius Clay (later Muhammad Ali) silenced his critics by beating the mighty Sonny Liston to become the World Heavyweight Champion for the first time. From that moment, the strong, confident Ali became Dad's hero, and posters of him adorned our home.

London looked on as civil rights leader Martin Luther King Jr addressed a congregation of 4,000 in St Paul's Cathedral – on his way to Stockholm to receive the Nobel Peace Prize. At a press conference following the service, King said,

There are growing racial problems in Britain as a result of the large number of coloured persons from the West Indies, from Pakistan and from India who are coming into the country. And it is my feeling that if Britain is not eternally vigilant, and if England does not in a real sense, go all out to deal with the problem now, it can mushroom and become as serious as the problem we face in some other Nations.[24]

When parents of my generation looked to us, their expectations took them away from the manual or unskilled work, as they hoped for their children to become doctors, lawyers, teachers. We were to step to the next level and fulfil their dreams. I became a part of my parents' dream when I was born on a bright Sunday morning in June, the third child to Waldes and Gwendoline Campbell. My sister Joyce was a year older, and my eldest sister Anne was born in Jamaica before my parents came to Britain. She lived in Jamaica with my grandmother.

Just four months after my birth, on 15 October, 1964, 16,690 British voters were to secure the Smethwick seat in Parliament for Peter Griffiths, riding on the back of the slogan, 'If you want a nigger for a neighbour vote Labour.'[25] Although Griffiths was not responsible for coining the phrase, he refused to disown it. 'I would not condemn any man who said that,' he told *The Times* during his election campaign. 'I regard it as a manifestation of popular feeling.'[26] People like me were to play a leading role in his maiden speech to the Commons as he blamed the immigrant communities for the problems his constituency faced, including factory closures and over 4,000 families awaiting council accommodation.[27]

A photograph of me as a baby hangs on the wall at my parents' home, alongside photos of my siblings. I am wrapped in white, and my mouth is slightly twisted as if I am about to cry. I love that photograph, not just because it's a part of my history, but because I was oblivious to the hate and resentment all around me at the time. *There was no fear.* To Griffiths and those like him, I was 'a nigger', but to my parents I was simply their baby girl, a blank canvas for whom anything was possible.

But there was hope for my generation, a political awareness making it clear that for us things had to be different, and racism would not be tolerated. Labour Prime Minister Harold Wilson stated at the Labour Party Conference in 1965, 'Everyone living in this country, everyone who has come in, or will come in, is a British citizen, entitled to equality of treatment regardless of origin or race or colour.'[28]

Hearing these strong words, our parents were bound to feel optimism and to believe that, over time, the evils of racism – endemic in their lives, denying them decent accommodation, skilled work and bank accounts – would cease to exist and the signs displayed in windows across Britain reading 'No Irish, No Blacks, No Dogs' would become a thing of the past. But, no matter how well meaning Wilson's words were, was it too late for the West Indian community who had entered a war-torn Britain? London alone suffered 18,091 high explosions, 71 major air raids and 47,314 destroyed homes during the Second World War, the effects of which were exacerbated by the rationing of building materials that did not end until 1954–5.[29] Wilson failed to take account of the fact that there had been no infrastructure in place to accommodate those arriving from the Caribbean. Wilson talked about the need for integration, but how was that possible when exclusions led to a separation of the Black community? West Indians had no choice but to set up their own clubs in which to socialise, play their music and enjoy a drink.

Dad came to Britain in the hope of starting his own business, something a bank loan would have helped him to do. But because West Indians were more often than not denied bank accounts with financial institutions, they had to create their own form of saving, known as the Paadna. A group of people agreed to pay a regular sum to a trusted person, such as an elderly member of the community. Every week, one member of the group received the total amount (called 'the draw'). It could be £50, £100, or whatever figure was agreed and could run from six weeks to six months, or even yearly. Dad joined a Paadna after getting his first job and used his first draw to send for Mum.

Joyce and I, both born in Hackney Hospital, lived with our parents in one room in a large house in Hackney. Joyce would sleep in the bed with Mum and Dad, and I in the cot. I am relieved that we were both too young to remember those days, because we were sharing the house with four other families; there was one kitchen and one bathroom. Back in the 1960s, you had to put money in a meter for gas. Mum told me horror stories of how, as soon as she put the money in, someone else would use the cooker and the gas would have run out by the time she got to the kitchen. I tried to get Mum to tell me more, but, like most of her generation, she was made of strong stock, so all she said was, 'It was hard.'

As far as some white public opinion was concerned, my family and other West Indians and all non-white people lived in these conditions by choice and were dirty and unhygienic. 'They've got some terrible habits . . . they leave their children on the pavement to do their business . . . I don't think they know what toilets are for.'[30] This comment and the many like it – one person even going so far as to say Black people eat cat food and dog food – should have been treated as laughable and dismissed as the product of attitudes at that time. But they were not something I could forget about and brush under the carpet, because these white people actually believed that what they were saying was true. It was an effrontery that people could think of my parents and family in this way, with no acknowledgement of the obstacles that they faced in trying to sustain a decent standard of living. How dare they say this about my mum and dad and those like them? What terrifies me is that, even though I was there, I was not aware of the prejudice. Mum and Dad had to deal with it head-on, and the more I learn, the more I understand why they chose not to talk about it.

However, post-war Britain made a mammoth move towards fairer treatment of the wider population from an economic and health perspective through the creation of the Welfare State. Not only was there now a National Health Service, but also, crucially, the 1944 Education Act established free secondary education for all. As children born in this country, we had an automatic entitlement to welfare services, and the most important of these for my parents was access to education.

But something more tangible than mere words was required from Harold Wilson and the Labour government to ensure equality for those of us who were settled here, and, before I took my first steps, the 1965 Race Relations Act was introduced. It was the first piece of legislation in the United Kingdom to make it unlawful to discriminate on grounds of race, colour or ethnic origin in public places. The purpose of the Race Relations Board, set up a year later, was to assess and resolve individual cases of discrimination, and committees were established across England, Wales and Scotland to receive and investigate complaints. However, the Act was restricted in a number of ways. It did not apply to employment, private accommodation, social housing or financial institutions, which gave carte blanche to landlords and banks to continue to deny us the right to decent accommodation, equal employment rights, loans or mortgages.

But a Black community enthused and revitalised by the civil rights movement in the United States and the visit of Martin Luther King Jr in 1964 began to create pressure groups for stronger legislation, the kind that would effectively untie our hands and give us a fighting chance. The Campaign Against Racial Discrimination (CARD) was one such group, chaired by Dr David Pitt, who lobbied for legislation that would place me on an equal footing with my white peers in the country of my birth.

I was not quite two when the Home Secretary Roy Jenkins prepared Britain for greater protection of immigrant communities. In his lecture on Roy Jenkins, Professor Vernon Bogdanor described him as 'the only really liberal Home Secretary that Labour has ever produced'.[31] On 23 May, 1966, Jenkins delivered a speech on race relations, widely considered one of his best, which was to pre-empt the 1968 Race Relations Bill. Jenkins argued that integration relied on equal opportunity, cultural diversity and mutual tolerance, saying, 'If discrimination were to happen to the rest of us, to the Welsh (like myself), to the Scots, to the Irish, to the Jews, to the mid-European, and to still more recent arrivals, it would be little short of a national disaster.'[32] Were we finally on our way to political change within Britain, change that would prohibit discrimination not only in housing, employment and public places, but also in banking and education, and bring an end to the 'No Coloureds' notices?

Surely this legislation would be the stepping stone towards ensuring the equality I and those like me had a right to expect as we entered our education and embarked on our chosen career paths. The world was changing, and Britain seemed to be following that change. The United States passed the Civil Rights Act of 1968, expanding on the 1964 Civil Rights Act, which prohibited discrimination based on race, colour, religion, sex or national origin by federal and state governments. The Civil Rights Act of 1968 prohibited discrimination concerning the sale, rental and financing of housing based on race, religion, national origin, sex and (as amended) disability.

Even though this was happening thousands of miles away across the Atlantic, the advancement of equality through political means in the United States was like a beacon of hope to Black people living in Britain. The 1965 Race Relations Act had been in place for three years, but it had made little or no difference to the Black community. It was still impossible for Dad to secure decent housing for his family, and we remained in cramped accommodation. Despite the 1968 Civil Rights Act taking over two years to pass in the United States, it gave hope to the Black community that Britain would follow suit in respect of the 1968 Race Relations Bill.

I am not naive enough to believe that a piece of legislation could have miraculously propelled the Black community on to an equal footing with whites and dispelled discrimination overnight, but like the Act in the United States, it was an important step on the road to change. It was meant to make a difference and result in a real push for change, something I know my parents and other West Indians prayed for to ease the discrimination they were experiencing.

We were unaware that there was someone who vehemently opposed any move towards legislative change, and that he would be prepared to do anything to make his voice heard.

ENOCH POWELL'S QUEST FOR IM— MORTALITY

CHAPTER
IV

'The task of the politician is to provide people with words and ideas which will fit their predicament, better than the words and ideas that they are using at the moment.' [33]
Enoch Powell

For years Enoch Powell was silent on the subject of race in Britain. MP for Wolverhampton from 1950, he maintained that silence despite the rise of right-wing extremism in the 1950s, the Notting Hill race riots, the death of Kelso Cochrane, the voices of MPs calling for restrictions on immigration. Why was he silent for so long? Because Enoch Powell was a strategist: it was not the right time to speak out about race, and he was a man who wanted to ensure that when he finally did speak out it would have the biggest impact on the white British population, propelling him to prominence, establishing his racist ideals, within UK politics. The most devastating element of his calculation was that he used the Black community, *my community*, to achieve this end.

On Saturday 20 April, 1968, two weeks after Martin Luther King Jr was assassinated, and three days before the debate of the 1968 Race Relations Bill that proposed to make it illegal to refuse housing, employment, or public services to people of colour, Powell, during a meeting of the Conservative Political Centre at the Midland Hotel, Birmingham, got to his feet at 2.30 p.m. and said, 'A week or two ago I fell into conversation with a constituent, a middle-aged man . . . an ordinary working man . . . who said, "In this country in fifteen or twenty years' time the Black man will have the whip hand over the white man."'[34]

Powell was specific in his attack, aiming directly at *people like Dad*, those Black men, and women, who had settled here with few or no rights. Powell knew that no one wanted to give up privilege, no matter how small – a privilege as simple as Dad taking the initiative on a building site to move a lorry out of the way, only to be told, 'What you doing in there, get out, that's not your job.' To that racist white workman, even the task of driving a lorry elevated Dad to a position of equality that induced fear. This was at the heart of Powell's rhetoric, his aim being to destroy any hope of integration, by alleging people like Dad received preferential treatment at work. Saying, 'To the immigrant, entry to this country was admission to privileges and opportunities eagerly sought, the impact upon the existing [white] population was very different . . . At work they found that employers hesitated to apply to the immigrant worker the standards of discipline and competence required of the native-born worker.'[35] But there was also a deliberate callousness in Powell's link to Britain's colonial power with his constituent's reference to 'the whip', an evil symbol synonymous with slavery. The crack of the whip was an audible threat to enslaved workers, keeping them at their labours and reminding them that their lives and bodies were not their own. That they should remain *subordinate*. Tears well up within me when I think about my dad, a strong, powerful, and proud man, being treated in such a despicable way, a white workman cracking the whip that day on the building site.

The calculation in Powell's use of this word was a message to the Black community, his way of reminding us of our past. A past filled with violence and heinous crimes against humanity carried out by the white man, *the master*. Effectively, what Powell was telling the Black community in 1968 was the white man *did* have the whip hand over the Black man. And that's how he wanted it to stay, because in Powell's eyes people of colour would never be equal to the white man, saying: 'Where there are marked differences, especially of colour, integration is difficult though, over a period, not impossible. There are among the Commonwealth immigrants who have come here... whose wish and purpose is to be integrated and whose every thought and endeavour is bent in that direction. But to imagine such a thing enters the heads of a great and growing majority of immigrants and their descendants is a ludicrous misconception, and a dangerous one.'[36]

Powell went on to state, 'The Commonwealth immigrant came to Britain as a full citizen, to a country which knew no discrimination between one citizen and another, and he entered instantly into the possession of the rights of every citizen, from the vote to free treatment under the National Health Service.'[37]

'Possession of the rights' – what rights? It's difficult to come to terms with a statement that is so misleading. On paper there may have been no discrimination between one citizen and another, as far as the right to vote and welfare services were concerned, but the discrimination that existed within the hearts and minds of British society was very real. Take the Notting Hill riots, the death of Kelso Cochrane, the lack of protection provided to the Black community and the ongoing prejudice within the police force. These were the race-related restrictions that existed throughout the country. Powell deliberately closed his mind to the injustices that the Black community were suffering, deflecting that injustice on to white people by accusing Black people of being a drain on public services and a threat to British society.

But people like me had been born here, had become a part of British society: surely *my generation* could be the ones to forge an alliance between white and Black communities? But to Powell we were the most dangerous of all.

At three years old I was blissfully unaware of the infamous 'Rivers of Blood' speech of 20 April, 1968, that built to a crescendo of resentment against the Black community, with my generation being described as 'wide-grinning piccaninnies'. Reading the speech years later, I felt hurt at the damage Powell had done. It was an out-and-out attack on a community that had no voice of their own in Parliament or economic standing within Britain. Powell was kicking us when we were already down, because in his mind that was the best time to do it.

But why were we such a threat? To Powell, 'Elevating the immigrant and his descendants into a privileged or special class . . . was establishing a one-way act of privilege by an act of Parliament.'[38]

The impact of Powell's speech on the Black community was far-reaching, with the most regrettable aspect of it being the erosion of trust between them and the white community. Dad found it so hard to feel safe around white people. Over time he might have mellowed were it not for Powell's speech, which destroyed his hope of finding a positive way forward. I asked Mum what the Black community did after the speech and she simply said, 'What could we do?'

My uncle and his family lived in Wolverhampton at the time and were a part of Powell's constituency. When I asked him how the Black community coped, he said, 'When we walked past his headquarters we walked on the other side of the road.'

This resilience made my parents' generation stronger than anything Enoch Powell could throw at them, no matter how ruthless his intentions were.

I try to imagine what the atmosphere must have been like. If Black people had white friends, what did they do? Black and white people clearly worked together: how did Powell's speech affect their working life? However, Mum and Dad, like the rest of the West Indian community, didn't scream or shout about it; instead, they continued to work, keep a roof over our heads, clothe us and put food on the table.

After the speech, Powell was dismissed from the Shadow Cabinet by the Conservative party leader Edward Heath, who stated, 'I consider the speech he made in Birmingham yesterday to have been racialist in tone and liable to exacerbate racial tensions.'[39] But Powell's sacking had a snowball effect, as the speech generated much correspondence to newspapers, markedly in Wolverhampton, whose sorting office received 40,000 postcards and 8,000 letters addressed to its local newspaper, the *Express & Star*. Ninety-five per cent of them were pro-Powell and offering support.[40] This politician had captured the mood of the white British public and became one of the most popular politicians in Britain.

In the immediate aftermath of Powell's speech and dismissal, 4,000 London and Tilbury dockers stopped work and 800 of their number marched from the East End to the Palace of Westminster carrying placards, as did Smithfield meat porters in their bloody overalls.

A Gallup poll showed that 75 per cent of the population were sympathetic to Powell's views.[41] A National Opinion Poll (NOP) showed that approximately 75 per cent of the British population agreed with Powell's demand for non-white immigration to be halted completely, and about 60 per cent agreed with his inflammatory call for the repatriation of non-whites already resident in Britain.[42]

Powell had planted a seed that was all too willing to grow within the hearts and minds of the white population. The Labour MP Richard Crossman noted that Powell had 'stirred up the nearest thing to a mass movement since the 1930s . . . Enoch is stimulating the real revolt of the masses . . . he has changed the whole shape of politics overnight.'[43]

On 23 April, 1968, the Race Relations Bill had its second reading in the House of Commons. Powell was present for the debate, but did not speak. The Act became law on 25 October, 1968.

On the day Powell made his speech he broke the law, because under Incitement to Racial Hatred, Section 6 of the 1965 Race Relations Act states, 'A person shall be guilty of an offence . . . if, with intent . . . he uses in any public place or at any public meeting words which are threatening, abusive or insulting, being matter or words likely to stir up hatred against that section on grounds of colour, race, or national origins.'

Labour MP Edward Leadbitter stated he would refer the speech to the Director of Prosecutions, and the Liberal Party leader Jeremy Thorpe spoke of a prima facie case against Powell for incitement. But these were empty words, as no legal action was taken against him, despite the fact that, just a year before, the leader of the White Defence League Colin Jordan had been sent to prison for eighteen months for distributing leaflets on 'the Black invasion' and incitement.

By escaping prosecution, Powell had effectively legitimised right-wing views that would have a ripple effect on me and my community for years to come. Bearing Powell's popularity in mind, I am not surprised no politician stepped forward to report Powell to the police and push for a prosecution against him: it would have been a courageous move, as it would have meant political suicide. Risking everything for the Black community was not something these politicians were prepared to do.

Although Powell had destroyed any chance, he had of achieving a ministerial position, he continued in his role as a Member of Parliament and enjoyed all the rights and protection that went with it. But who would protect us from his rhetoric?

There is no doubt that prejudice existed in Britain long before Enoch Powell delivered his speech, but any hope of us being given equal access to all aspects of British life was sabotaged by Powell's calculated move. In ensuring he made the biggest splash possible; he convinced the majority of the white population that any extension of the 1968 Race Relations Act would have provided my generation with *privilege rather than equality*,

and the most damaging aspect of this belief has been its lon-
gevity. It has run like an invisible thread through every aspect
of British society for decades, meaning that any policies or
employment practices designed to address the racial imbalance
through positive affirmative action are often met with disdain.
It's as if the attempts to level the playing field are seen as giving
people a way in through the back door on racial grounds, a way
in that – in some people's eyes – we do not deserve, despite our
credentials.

In October 2019, top-ranked solicitors in Manchester and
London, Leigh Day, advertised apprenticeships specifically for
Black people in a bid to increase the number of Black lawyers
it employed. The firm's campaign stated that it was looking for
those who had completed their A levels 'to a good grade', and
who wished to become solicitors without going to university.
Frances Swaine, Leigh Day's managing partner, said the firm
had fewer Afro-Caribbean and African qualified staff 'than we
ought to have for our geographical area'.[44] She said the firm
was failing to attract enough trainee applications from Black
candidates, and so it had decided to take direct action and
recruit at a student level. The reaction from those working in
the legal profession to the positive steps taken was it may cause
resentment, 'It's like opening a Pandora's box.'[45]

But why should it cause resentment, when all that is being done is levelling the playing field? Is striving for equality
wrong? The same argument is used time after time: it should
be about 'merit'. When a person of colour obtains a job through
positive action, there is a presumption that they are not the best
person for the job, despite their having the qualifications and
being equally capable.

A recent study from Nuffield College, University of Oxford,[46]
confirmed five decades of previous research, showing that
ethnic minorities have to send in 60 per cent more CVs even
when they have the same qualifications as white applicants,

which evidences that discrimination within the labour market has barely changed over fifty years. A report published in June 2019 from the Bar Standards Board also found evidence of discrimination.[47] Figures showed that ethnic minority students were less likely to get a pupillage than white students with similar levels of academic attainment, with 44 per cent of white students starting pupillages, compared to 23 per cent of the ethnic minority. In 1968, Enoch Powell condemned recruitment drives like Leigh Day's for 'elevating the immigrant and his descendants into a privileged or special class'.[48]

However, to truly understand Powell's motivation for making his speech all those years ago, we need to return to 1939, just a year before the young man joined the Army. Powell published a book titled *A Lexicon to Herodotus* that detailed every word the Greek historian – considered the 'Father of History' – had written, and their origins.[49] In writing the book, Professor Bogdanor stated in his lecture that Powell had said that he hoped it 'would secure him immortality . . . preserve his name even if as he expected he was killed in the war'.[50]

Today, when people speak about Enoch Powell, little is said about his classical work. Fifty years on, he is remembered for his 'Rivers of Blood' speech that has secured his place in British history. He achieved his wish for immortality after all, but did so off the back of stirring up racial hatred against the Black community.

A
CHANGE
OF
POSTCODE

CHAPTER
V

At five years old, the boundaries of my life had been clearly drawn. When white people saw me, they would not see a child. To them, I, and those like me, represented a threat to their well being and future opportunities. I was heading into a battle-field, as Powell's unconscionable, uncensored barrage provided a great boost for the far right. A. K. Chesterton, cousin of G. K. Chesterton and founder of the National Front, considered Powell's views as National Front policy, paving the way for a legitimate entry into the political arena.

In 1969, Enoch Powell's notoriety was to take him across the Atlantic to America despite his concerns about the 'special re-lationship' between Britain and the USA, a country he believed was keen to see the end of the British Empire.[51] Powell appeared on *The Firing Line*, an American public affairs show founded and hosted by prominent and influential conservative author and columnist William F. Buckley Jr. who in 1957 wrote a piece for the *National Review* called 'Why the South Must Prevail'. In this article, Buckley contended that white Southerners were entitled to 'take such measures as . . . necessary to prevail, po-litically and culturally, over Black citizens'.[52]

Powell's TV interview took place in my first year of primary school, when I had no understanding of what was meant by the term 'a wide-grinning piccaninny'. I lived my life much like any other child. I played, laughed, and cried, mixing with boys and girls, Black and white, with whom I would spend the next six years of my young life. But during that interview, Powell expressed his fervent belief that, irrespective of my education, and immersion in British culture, my skin colour would always be a barrier that I and my white friends would never be able to overcome, despite my ability: 'Colour is a signal, an outward signal of differences, and it signifies other differences that one can't deny.'[53] I had no idea that in Powell's eyes, and in the eyes of those who followed him, I and those like me were being set apart from our white peers, for no other reason than for the colour of our skin.

But despite the ongoing influence of Powell, my family continued to live in Britain and our parents protected us from the racism that existed all around us. I don't remember the day we moved to Spring Hill. Mum tells me it was in the late 1960s, before my two brothers were born, and Dad said it was the beginning of a change in our lives. Spring Hill was a quiet area in Clapton, East London, that overlooked Springfield Park. There was no poor social housing. We were the only Black family on the street and lived on the first floor of a two-storey house, surrounded by Orthodox Jews. I spent eight years of my life at Spring Hill. The park was our garden; my sister and I would play at the front so that Mum could stick her head out of the window and tell us when it was time to come in. We played together with the Jewish children. When my two brothers Fitz and Glen came along in 1968 and 1970, we all played there together as a family. The primary school, which I loved, was only fifteen minutes away.

I can only imagine how my parents must have felt, moving into a street where we were effectively on our own, without the comfort blanket of others from our community, but Dad said he saw a chance and no matter how it turned out he was prepared to take it. And looking back, we were living among people who had suffered some of the worst human rights atrocities in history. Jewish people knew what it was like to suffer the degradation of racism, and felt safe in their own community. They did not bother us, and we did not bother them. Those first few years of my life moulded me into who I am now, because for years we grew up away from any prejudice.

However, some landlords would adopt practices of letting their properties to Black people, so that rent-controlled white tenants would feel they had little choice but to leave. This enabled the landlords to let out their flats at a higher rate. When we moved into Spring Hill, there was a Jewish lady living downstairs. She was a lovely lady, who worked in a cake shop on the high street. Every night she would call me or Joyce downstairs and hand us a bag of doughnuts. When we left, eight years later, she was still there. Eventually, we discovered that we were only moved in so that she would move out. But she didn't move out, and instead she and my mother became good friends. We would play with her grandson, who visited her regularly, and when we finally moved to our first house in Tottenham, she would come and visit us.

The one time I did experience prejudice whilst living in Spring Hill, I only recognised it in retrospect. I had a white friend. We were in the same class at primary school. She lived at the bottom of the road, so I could see her house from our front-room window. One day when we were playing together in the park she fell and cut her knee and started crying. I took her to my house. Mum brought her into the kitchen, sat her down, cleaned her bloody knee and put a plaster on it. Then she gave each of us a doughnut and a drink, and we went back out to play. A few months later the same friend had a birthday party, but I was not invited. On the day of her party, there was non-stop excited chatter as all my classmates couldn't wait for classes to end. As I made my way home, I watched them pile into parents' cars. I spent the entire evening looking out the front-room window, wishing with all my heart that I was at the party. Mum looked on, shaking her head, just telling me 'it was a shame'. I was filled with confusion. It never entered my head that I hadn't been invited because I was Black. But if I were to try and describe how I felt, it would be that I was consumed with an agonising, painful disappointment that never quite went away.

Thankfully, Spring Hill was packed with so many good memories that these outweigh the bad. The books that provided me with the gift of reading were the Janet and John, Kathy and Mark early learning books, whose white characters played significant roles in my young life. One of my favourites was the Milly-Molly-Mandy series, illustrated short stories about a little girl in a pink-and-white striped dress. I read every one of the books cover to cover — I could not get enough of them. I was always the first to finish them in class. Milly-Molly-Mandy was white, but as far as I was concerned she was just like me.

My love of reading was clear to me from the beginning, something British education encouraged when I was at primary school. To my parents, education was the single most important aspect of living in Britain. I couldn't wait to learn to read. Before I could even string words together on a page, I would make up stories using Mum's catalogues, and I wasted no time when I started school, soaking up knowledge like a sponge.

One day, out of the blue, when I was eight years old, my teachers called me into the staff room and asked me to read from a sheet of paper. I was told I had been selected with some of the older children to join a choral speaking team, a literacy technique where students read passages together. We practised every week and worked really hard to be the best we could be, in preparation for the competition against different schools across the country.

My parents were so proud, and I was excited beyond belief when Mum took me shopping for the uniform we had to wear. When the day arrived, I had to go home early and change. Dad was at work, but Mum got me ready – she was even more nervous than I was — and the Jewish lady who lived downstairs helped me with my tie.

When we arrived at the venue, there were so many other children. I was one of the youngest in the team but can still remember how thrilled I was. When we finally got to perform, we did everything exactly as we should; our teachers smiled and prompted us in the right places. Then came the results, which was a torturous wait, and I held on to my classmate: third . . . second . . . in first place . . . We won! It was brilliant. When we got on that stage to collect our trophy, our teachers' faces beamed. Mum, well, she started crying when I told her, and when Dad came home from work covered in plaster after working on a building site all day, I ran out to tell him before he even got into the house.

'We won, Daddy!' I shouted.

'What, yu win?!' he said with a massive smile as I followed him in.

My teachers told my parents I had a gift for the English language. 'Your daughter will go far,' they said.

I felt good, part of the British society in which I lived. There was no reason for me to believe that I didn't belong there.

THE IMMIGRATION ACT 1971 & ERIC CLAPTON, THE MAN WHO SHOT THE SHERIFF

CHAPTER
VI

In 1970, the same year my brother Glen was born, the Conservatives had a surprise victory in the general election over Harold Wilson's Labour government, a win that was due, in part, to the right-wing support for Enoch Powell and his hostility towards non-white immigration. Commenting on the election, the American pollster, Douglas Schoen and University of Oxford academic, R. W. Johnson believed it 'beyond doubt' that Powell had attracted 2.5 million votes to the Conservatives.[54] In Powell's own constituency at the 1970 election, his majority of 26,252 and a 64.3 per cent share of the vote were the highest of his career.[55] It had become a key factor in swaying votes, and, under growing pressure from Powell and the Powellites, the new Home Secretary Reginald Maudling announced the creation of the Immigration Bill 1971. The Bill clamped down on the flow of 'new Commonwealth' immigrants arriving in Britain – which included those from countries in the West Indies, Africa, Asia and India – whilst simultaneously introducing 'open door' concessions for citizens of the 'old Commonwealth' countries, namely Australia, New Zealand, Canada and South Africa, who were of 'British stock'.[56] The Tory government effectively exempted 70 per cent of the 'white' Commonwealth from any immigration curbs.[57]

I was almost seven years old when, in April 1971, 3,000 people marched through the City of London to hand a memorandum to the Prime Minister Edward Heath that protested against the

1971 Immigration Bill, stating, 'The Bill creates insecurity in the lives of immigrants . . . and will also help to persuade the British people that Black people are second-class and undesirable.'[58] But despite concerns raised by the West Indian Organisations, Indians and Pakistanis, the Bill was made into law on 28 October, 1971 and remains in force to this day.

In May 1971, Powell appeared on Dick Cavett's popular talk show in America and said:

In 1962 at last, the law was changed so as to make a difference between British subjects who belonged to this country and those that don't. But by the time that had happened, so large a number had settled here . . . that we now know unless drastic change happens, large parts of many of our cities will, by the beginning of the next century, be occupied by a population which has nothing in common with the people of this country.[59]

It's hard to see how a man who was considered intellectually gifted could be so blinkered. Powell was always very careful only to refer to the influx of immigrants into Britain, and what he saw as the detrimental effect that would have on the British white community by the beginning of the next century. But no reference was made in his 1968 speech, or any that followed, to those from the white British population who were emigrating to other countries. A report published in December 2006 by Public Policy Research found that while Britons have been moving all around the world for centuries, the scale of emigration from the UK in recent years has been staggering. Over the 39 years between 1966 and 2005, the UK experienced a total loss of some 2.7 million British nationals. In other words, every year for the past 39 years, around 67,500 more British left the UK than came back in the UK. The report also showed that in 2005, for example, 198,000 Britons left to start new lives abroad, while 91,000 came back to the UK. An estimated 5.5 million British people live permanently abroad. In addition, an estimated 500,000 British people live abroad for part of the year – mainly through second-home ownership – which equates to almost one in ten British nationals.[60] The emigration of British people has happened in cycles over 200 years. The trend is now rising again: some 2,000 British citizens moved permanently away from the UK every week in 2005.[61]

According to the website of Spain's Secretary of State for Migration, the number of UK citizens with Spanish residence permits increased by 8.2 per cent from June 2018 to June 2019.[62] The rate then rose a further 5.8 per cent from June 2019 to June 2020, an increase of 19,977 British residents. In the Spanish island of Menorca, which has a population of only 96,000 (4,000 of whom are British residents), a further 300 UK citizens have applied for residency since the summer of 2019.[63]

Britons then and now continue to take advantage of the opportunity to settle permanently in other parts of the world, but is that deemed acceptable only because many who are choosing to do so are white? Do those who become 'ex-pats' contribute in any way to the new communities in which they live? Do they have anything in common with the Spanish, for instance? Do they speak the language?

In introducing this Bill, the government was guilty of racism. Once in place, the Act was a reflection of the growing political influence of Enoch Powell on immigration policy, his popularity within the media in Britain and the United States, and with extreme right-wing groups, such as the emerging National Front. But why should I and my family, or any other West Indians already settled in the UK, have worried? This new legislation did not apply to us. But by making the distinction between Black and white Commonwealth members, the government sent a clear message to the white British public that people of colour were not welcome in Britain. And Powell's demands for repatriation for those of us already here had a powerful impact. It tainted the Black and Brown population as, regardless of whether we were born here or held British passports, we were frowned upon by the white population. But life went on – Joyce, Fitz and I went to school, mixed with our Black and white classmates and our parents continued to work.

Immigration was not the only topic to take centre stage in the 1970s. Campaigners who had fought for women's equality saw the introduction of Equal Pay Act 1970, which prohibited unfavourable treatment of women in terms of pay and conditions of employment. Although women had managed to secure further working conditions, the immigrant communities still faced discrimination within the workplace and it was clear that stronger legislation was required to combat this.

By my twelfth birthday, a year after I started secondary school, the newly formed Labour government introduced the Race Relations Act 1976, which extended discrimination to include indirect discrimination consisting of where everyone is treated the same, but there are conditions or requirements which put members of a particular racial group at a disadvantage compared with others and which cannot be justified on non-racial grounds.[64] Once again, it was Home Secretary Roy Jenkins taking the lead, stating in Parliament, 'The success of legislation depends on the one hand upon the leadership of government and Parliament and on the other hand upon the response of society as a whole . . . These measures are needed not only to combat discrimination and encourage equal opportunity but also to tackle what has come to be known as 'racial disadvantage.'[65]

But what would make this Act any different to the others that had preceded it? Any change required innovative thinking and commitment, a flexible mind and willingness to adapt. For the 1976 Act to have any real effect, change had to come from within. The problem was the same – employers, unions, teachers, housing providers were still in place, and government officials could not police factory floors, housing offices, schools. Powellites, members of the National Front or those who sympathised with their views and opposed equality for the Black community were embedded within every aspect of British society and, as such, would be likely to have undue influence within work and housing environments. How easy would it be to identify those factions?

The government also had to look to themselves. They were taking steps to try and alleviate discrimination, yet the country's own immigration policies had created a clear distinction between whites and people of colour through the implementation of the 1971 Immigration Act. The irony was not lost on me that there were in fact no MPs from ethnic minorities at that time, which illustrated how racial disadvantage had seeped into all levels of British society, including the heart of government.

Support for Enoch Powell was not limited to the Powellites and other right-wingers; he was also to find an ally in the world of rock music. On 5 August, 1976, whilst on stage at the Birmingham Odeon, a drunk Eric Clapton ranted to an audience of 2,000 rock fans. [66] He called for 'foreigners' 'wogs' and 'fucking Jamaicans' not just to 'leave the hall' but to 'leave [the] country' as he spoke in favour of Enoch Powell's 'Rivers of Blood' speech.'[67] Clapton warned fans that the country was in danger of becoming 'a Black colony within ten years'. What made Clapton's racist views even more astonishing was that, as an internationally renowned rock star, he had forged his musical career through the blues – the music of the Black man, music borne out of slavery. Clapton had made his entire living from appropriating African American culture.

Clapton's racist abuse was to have far-reaching effects, not just from the perspective of other musicians, but from that of the young people who followed his music and were influenced by him. Successful Black writer Caryl Phillips was just eighteen at the time and had attended the concert with his white friend.

It wasn't unusual for him to be the only Black person in the audience, but, when Clapton started telling the audience that Powell was right, Phillips felt uncomfortable:

> **I felt embarrassed, and I could tell my friend felt embarrassed...Possibly the worst part was the ride home, on the top deck of the bus with my friend. We couldn't really talk about it; something had come between our friendship. The friendship never recovered, to tell the truth. We didn't have the vocabulary as seventeen/eighteen-year-old kids to actually put into context what had just happened. It was too shocking. It was a betrayal...I went home, I never spoke about it to my brothers, never spoke about it to my parents. It never came up at school the next day. I never wanted to listen to Eric Clapton again.**[68]

Phillips' experience shows how destructive racism can be. What makes it even more insidious is how hard it is to talk about it, and how not talking about it that can lead to damaged relationships between Black people and white people. Eric Clapton was a revered musician who had fans all over the world. He had just had a hit with Bob Marley's, 'I Shot the Sheriff'. As with Enoch Powell, no action was taken against Clapton for his racist abuse, which would have amounted to racial incitement at that time.

And, although his words were to be the catalyst for the Rock Against Racism movement in 1976 – a national campaign that lasted for five years, and for part of which musicians held concerts and rallies throughout the country – Eric Clapton continued to excel in his career as a successful musician. In 1994 he was awarded an OBE for services to music, was inducted into the Rock and Roll Hall of Fame for the third time in 2000 and received a CBE from the Princess Royal at Buckingham Palace in 2004.

Caryl Phillips went on to become an award-winning author and playwright. His novels uncover the experiences of the peoples of the African diaspora in England, the Caribbean, and the United States. But, unlike Clapton, he is yet to receive a CBE.

'RULE BRITANNIA!'

CHAPTER VII

The year was 1977 and it was the day of my thirteenth birthday. My parents bought me a Timex watch to mark the occasion. By then my sister Joyce, brothers Fitz and Glen and I had settled into our three-bedroom house in Tottenham. I was to share my day with another special event, as the country revelled in the euphoria of the bank holiday marking the Silver Jubilee of Queen Elizabeth II.

Crowds lined the route of the procession to St Paul's Cathedral, where the royal family attended a Service of Thanksgiving alongside many world leaders, including the President of the United States, Jimmy Carter and the UK Prime Minister James Callaghan, along with all of the living former Prime Ministers.

Towns and villages threw elaborate street parties, strung bunting from rooftop to rooftop. In London alone there were over 4,000 organised parties for individual streets and neighbourhoods.[69] Onlookers were greeted by Her Majesty the Queen as she made several appearances on the balcony of Buckingham Palace. In addition to throwing parties, many decorated motor vehicles evoking Britain's past, and drove them about town, organising their very own parades.

My family watched the revellers celebrating all things British. There was a fierce patriotism, with the flying of the Union Jack. But the revelry made me feel uneasy — patriotism in Britain had a way of excluding anyone who was different, not seen as *British*.

The celebrations were a welcome distraction from the financial crisis Britain was experiencing. The year before, the Labour government had been forced to borrow 3.9 billion dollars from the International Monetary Fund (IMF), which at the time was the largest loan ever to have been requested, because of the increase in world oil prices. But the loan came with strict conditions attached – the IMF demanded large cuts in public spending, which ended plans to expand the economy and improve social services. As inflation and unemployment increased, striking the heart of the working-class population, extreme right-wing groups like the National Front were quick to exploit the situation. Their membership swelled as the Black community and other immigrant communities were blamed for the loss of jobs and for being a drain on welfare services.

The Silver Jubilee year saw the National Front secure nearly 120,000 votes in local elections with a racist political campaign that continued to gain momentum. In Hackney South and Shoreditch, they managed to push the Liberals into fourth place, receiving 2,886 votes and taking 19 per cent overall, votes which previously would have gone to Labour. The message from the National Front was clear – stop immigration and start repatriation.[70]

Signs reading 'Wogs Out' were spread across walls and buildings in heavily populated immigrant areas. Places like Tower Hamlets were also to become a focus for the National Front. Tower Hamlets had always been a safe Labour seat, but with the closure of the London Docks in 1981, it had become run down as industry drifted away from the inner city. The borough housed a sizeable Asian immigrant population who had arrived in large numbers during the 1960s and 70s, and in 1977 the National Front had a newspaper pitch in Brick Lane 'supported' by skinhead newspaper sellers.[71]

The leader of the National Front was John Tyndall, and their policy was, 'The repatriation by the most humane means possible of those immigrants already here, together with their descendants and dependants.'[72] The aim was to send immigrant communities home, or, where that was not possible, to resettle us anywhere else in the world except Britain.

Asked whether he believed the white man to be 'ethnically superior', Tyndall responded, 'Yes, undoubtedly. I'm not talking about the white man in relation to for instance the Japanese or the Chinese. I'm talking about the white man in relation to the Negro.'[73]

Racial hatred was being legitimised in a way it had never been before, with extremists gaining a foothold within the political world. It didn't seem to matter that we were born here, or that our parents had worked hard, paid their taxes and helped to build Britain after the war. Because to the National Front and those like them, we were 'a problem' and unwanted in their country. Tyndall described himself as 'very patriotic'.[74] Like Enoch Powell, he was fervent in his love for Queen and Country. Patriotism is one of the most powerful weapons in the fight against Black and immigrant communities.

But the arguments levelled by these men who preached white supremacy were flawed, because they were built on the premise that only the British white man had a claim to British patriotism. Many of the Caribbean people who arrived on the *Windrush* had been stationed in Britain during the Second World War, men and women who were willing to fight and die for their King and Country. They did this despite the fact that, at the time of the First World War, British Secretary of State for War Lord Kitchener – whose face was on the poster proclaiming 'Your Country Needs You' – didn't want Black recruits. Kitchener was concerned, firstly that Black soldiers would be too visible on the battlefield and secondly, that in fighting alongside their white comrades, they would gain the confidence to demand freedom from the British Empire after the war.[75] But King George V wanted to show the world a united Empire in wartime and felt that the exclusion of Black troops might undermine British governance in the colonies. He overruled Kitchener and in October 1915 the British West Indies Regiment was formalised.[76]

It did not matter that the regiment were not given the same opportunities to fight alongside white soldiers, with the War Office limiting their participation to 'labour' duties. These duties required them to head to the Western Front, where they dug trenches, built roads and emplacements, acted as stretcher bearers, loaded ships and trains, and worked in ammunition dumps, work that was often carried out within the range of German artillery and snipers.[77] They escorted 4,000 prisoners of war from Italy to Egypt and subsequently the regiment undertook mine clearance around the Suez Canal.

An estimated 10,000 Black West Indian volunteers came to Britain to enlist in the Army, the Navy, and the Air Force individually, once the discriminatory restrictions in each service was lifted, which came in 1939 in the Army and Navy and in 1940 in the Air Force. Nearly 500 Black men from the West Indies, Africa and Britain answered the call to serve as aircrew, and thousands more worked as ground-support staff.

In addition, following the war Black people from across the Caribbean came to Britain *at the request of the British government to help rebuild the country,* leaving the homes and the families they knew behind.

As a child watching the Silver Jubilee celebrations, I couldn't help feeling excluded, because throughout all the revelry there were no Black faces; there was no recognition of my community's contribution to British society. The Black community should have held their own parties to shout from the rooftops that they along with the rest of the country were a part of British society, had fought in the wars alongside them, and shown Enoch Powell, John Tyndall and everyone like them, that they were not going anywhere. But with all history there will be parts that you will be proud of, and others that will take you to places you wished you never had to go.

ROOTS & THE MORANT BAY REBELLION

CHAPTER VIII

There are certain events in your life that you never forget, and because of their significance you remember precisely where you were at the time. For some, it's the day President Kennedy or Martin Luther King was assassinated, for others it's the terrible events of 9/11. For me, it was a spring evening in April 1977 when my parents sat me and my sister and brothers down in front of the television to watch the first screening of *Roots*, a series which told the story of Kunta Kinte, an eighteenth-century Mandinka tribesman abducted from his village and transported across the Atlantic as an enslaved person.

I watched in terror as they placed the shackles on him, and he struggled and fought to get free. I lay awake all night, relieved that the passage of time had given me a way out of slavery. *That I was free*. But even though I'd known about slavery, or at least had had an idea of it, seeing on that small colour TV this young Black tribesman being forcibly taken away from the life he knew resulted in a loss of innocence I would never get back.

My best friend was a white girl. We were extremely close and would tell each other everything, but after watching *Roots*, my attitude towards my friend changed. She was still *a good friend* – we looked out for each other. I never told her how I felt, but I saw her in a different light, because the rules that applied to her would never apply to me. That was my first real experience of how destructive racism could be. I tried to pretend I wasn't envious of her, of her long blonde hair and blue eyes, but I was. It hurt that she represented everything that I didn't.

I had never been into politics, but I started reading about apartheid in South Africa, because it was the closest thing to slavery I could think of. I would sit next to my friend in class, look around the room at the white students and think, *If we were in South Africa, I wouldn't be allowed in here*. Maybe it would have been good to talk to her about it, find out what she thought, but I was raw, confused, angry with white people. I tried not to be, but I could not help it. Was I being a racist, blaming white people for something their ancestors had done? Was I any different to people who were racist against me, just because of the colour of my skin? Dad always told us, if you're not sure about how you feel about something, 'Tink wid yu head and not yu heart.'

I wished one of my teachers had had the courage to discuss *Roots* with us or even ask us how we felt about it. Children like me were curious, wanted to know more, understand. I imagine that everyone in the Black community who had watched *Roots* on TV was affected by it, but none of my teachers ever spoke about it. I felt that they didn't care about what had happened to us, and it didn't matter to them. *We didn't matter to them*. But how easy would it have been to have had that conversation with my white teachers? How could they have explained to a thirteen-year-old Black child that more than 12 million Africans were abducted from their homes and families, made to undertake a voyage of weeks, chained in the dark aboard tiny heaving ships, packed in with hundreds of naked strangers, living, dying, dead. And that those who survived the voyage were faced with the prospect of being literally worked to death. And that this lasted for hundreds of years. When you consider it in those terms, it's understandable that it wasn't something they would have felt comfortable talking about.

My parents took each day in their stride, but making sure we watched *Roots* was their way of ensuring we knew about slavery and the impact it had on our ancestral past. Dad was always telling us about how important it was that we understood Black history, and watching *Roots*, no matter how distressing it was, gave me a taste for learning more about Jamaican history. I found a book on Jamaican uprisings during slavery and read all about the rebellion in Jamaica in 1831, when more than 20,000 rebels seized control of the island, setting planters' houses on fire. It took the British Army and militia a month to restore order. Two hundred enslaved Africans and 14 white people died in the fire. But at least 340 rebel slaves were hung or shot afterwards.

It was strange reading about Black people in a way I had never done before. Until that moment all the books I had read showed Black people as subservient, passive beings who just allowed things to happen to them. In the films on TV, Black people were either maids, cleaners, or station porters. But in reading about Jamaica, I uncovered the history of Black enslaved people, who were killed resisting embarkation or who fought for their freedom no matter what the consequences. Hundreds of slaves died in uprisings, their names lost.

As I read about Jamaican history, I came across some unexpected information that made me realise just how distorted British history can be, and which had a profound effect on my love of the English language. The Morant Bay Rebellion of 1865 was a revolt against dire living conditions and disenfranchisement of Black people under British colonial rule in the years following the end of slavery. Hundreds of Black peasants marched on the Morant Bay courthouse to protest low wages, high rents, and widespread poverty. High poll taxes meant that freed men couldn't vote, and Jamaican politics was overwhelmingly white. Led by Baptist deacon Paul Bogle, the crowds seized weapons and attacked the local police station and other premises.

The Governor of Jamaica, Edward John Eyre, declared martial law, which lasted for thirty days and used British troops and militia to crush the rebellion. Over 400 protesters and innocent people were killed, 600 were publicly flogged and 1,000 homes were burnt to the ground. William Gordon, a mixed-raced advocate for Black people who spoke out openly in opposition to Governor Eyre, was also arrested for inciting the rebellion, despite the fact he was not even in Morant Bay at the time. Eyre seized the opportunity to arrest Gordon, who, along with Bogle, was soon convicted and executed.

Black people were killed indiscriminately under martial law. Most of them had not been involved in either the riot at the courthouse or the later rebellion. According to one soldier, 'We killed all before us . . . man or woman or child.'[78] It was the most severe suppression of unrest in the history of the British West Indies, exceeding incidents during slavery years.

When news of the Jamaican government's response to the rebellion broke in Britain, it generated fierce debate. When Eyre returned to Britain in 1866, a number of unsuccessful prosecutions were brought against him for murder. But Eyre had some powerful supporters, including influential British historian Thomas Carlyle, a long list of peers, military officers, bishops and many conservative establishment figures.[79] In 1853 Carlyle had written the notorious and inflammatory article in a pamphlet, entitled 'Occasional Discourse on The Nigger Question', in which he made his position clear. He argued that slavery should never have been abolished and that the free Black man was no more than a lazy pumpkin eater whose place on the earth was to work for the white colonial landowners, and do so with the ability given to him and for no other purpose.[80]

One of the worst things in life is to lose faith in someone you admired for their talent. As a child I loved musicals. I would watch them avidly. Two of my all-time favourites are *Oliver!* released in 1968, and *Scrooge* released in 1970. Certain films stick in your mind and, for me, both of these stand the test of time, because they were gut wrenching extravaganzas with that all important happy ending. As a child, I would also lie under the covers and soak in works like *Great Expectations* and *David Copperfield*, novels written by a man long-since departed.

Therefore, there was an overwhelming disappointment when I discovered that, despite the weight of evidence against Eyre and the racist views held by Carlyle, Charles Dickens was part of the pro-Eyre committee and lent his name to his cause. Charles Dickens's works played a significant part in my enjoyment of reading and in expanding my literary knowledge and education. I am also aware that his depiction of Ebenezer Scrooge did much to publicise the plight of working-class people during the 1840s, which is commendable. As I researched those who supported Governor Eyre, and Dickens's name jumped out of the page at me, I was not sure what to do. Jamaica is my parents' birthplace – it's part of who I am. Should I continue to read his books, watch adaptations of his work? As with the horrors of slavery, I wanted to go back to that comfortable place where I was ignorant and Charles Dickens's name was not on that list.

On 9 June, 2020, Britain marked 150 years since the death of Charles Dickens. The Dean of Westminster laid a wreath and said prayers at the writer's grave. Dickens is revered all over the world. He is a key figure of British literature, and no matter what he did, nothing can take away what he has enabled me to achieve through reading his works, which is the biggest contradiction of all.

Things were so different when I was that child who watched *Roots* back in 1977. We did not have the phenomenon of the Internet, where, with a few clicks of a computer keyboard we could find articles, links to journals and books on any topic as a means to educate ourselves. And although *history* is the key to revealing who we are, in Britain the subject is only compulsory up to the age of fourteen.

In 2016, historians called for schools and colleges to take a more balanced 'warts and all' approach to teaching children about the British Empire and colonialism, following research that revealed more than four in ten Britons view the British Empire as a good thing and something to be proud of.[81] Dr Andrea

Major, associate professor in British colonial history, University of Leeds, also called for improved teaching about the British Empire. Major said that there is 'collective amnesia about the levels of violence, exploitation and racism in many aspects of imperialism, not to mention the various atrocities and catastrophes that were perpetrated, caused and exacerbated by British colonial policies and actions.' [82]

The Secret Teacher is the *Guardian*'s anonymous blog where teachers can tell it like it is. One such teacher wrote that a pupil asked how a new module on slavery was relevant to this country, and why should they be bothered about something that happened miles away to people who are long gone. But the teacher pointed out that it was a different story when lessons were about Winston Churchill and the Second World War.[83]

The thoughts of the above pupil were similar to my own. I was detached from slavery; it was a million miles from the life I knew. And it was only when I saw *Roots* that I realised how important this element of my history was. I think a lot of history teachers believe it's important that children receive a balanced view of history. Maybe my own teachers did back then, but now I'll never know.

After I'd seen *Roots*, it wasn't just the white world I looked at differently, it was *me*. In the eyes of the world I would always be tainted by the stigmatisation of slavery and the racist ideals attached to it, which meant that when I looked in the mirror as a thirteen-year-old girl, I didn't like the dark brown reflection that stared back at me, because what came with it brought nothing but pain.

KIDS' TV & FAMILY DAYS OUT

CHAPTER
IX

I don't know how many of my generation would openly admit that they wished they weren't Black. It was an awful time for me in my early teens in the late 70's. On the one hand, I loved my family and took a pride in my mixed Jamaican and English cultures, on the other, our clear lack of representation within the mainstream, and rhetoric from Enoch Powell demanding repatriation hanging over our heads made me feel deflated and excluded.

Children's TV programmes included an adaptation of Enid Blyton's *The Famous Five* stories, along with *Blue Peter*, *Screen Test* and *Rainbow,* to name just a few, but no one who appeared in these shows looked like me. This changed in 1978, as I watched a Black boy called Benny Green, playing an eleven-year-old boy, walk through the school gates in the first episode of *Grange Hill*. A BBC children's drama series created by Phil Redmond (also responsible for *Brookside* and *Hollyoaks*), it ran for twenty years, ending on 15 September, 2008, and during that time made child stars of Terry Sue-Patt (who played Benny Green) and Todd Carty (Tucker Jenkins), who later played Mark Fowler in *EastEnders*.

Grange Hill was the first TV drama to portray a multicultural secondary school in Britain. Colin Freeman of the *Telegraph* wrote a moving article on the impact of the series when, sadly, Terry Sue-Patt passed away in 2015. He wrote that seeing Benny walking through the school gates in 1978 was his first acquaintance with a British kid his own age who was Black. This would have been the case for many others in the Britain of the 1970s, especially in Scotland, where Freeman grew up; there was only one Black pupil in his entire primary school. 'Yes, on telly there were Derek Griffiths and Floella Benjamin, the two Black presenters on *Play School*. TV presenters still belonged to the world of grown-ups and teachers. Benny Green was different. He was our age and did the sort of things that we did: messing about with his mates, getting bored in class, and generally going through the other ups and downs of a 1970s childhood.'[84]

Freeman goes on to note, 'It's easy to forget in this era of satellite TV and watch-on-demand, that in those days, when there were only three channels, Tuesdays and Fridays revolved entirely around that 5 p.m. slot just after John Craven's *Newsround*, when *Grange Hill* came on. Later episodes of *Grange Hill* also showed that being Black and British wasn't always easy. The series with the bully Gripper Stebson, for example, was the first and only time that children like me learned about the wrongs of racism (we didn't get taught about it at school).' The TV drama had a lot more influence on Freeman on that particular issue than any amount of lecturing by some earnest race-relations type.

As a child, it would have been great to spend the summer jetting off to blue seas and sandy beaches like a lot of my white friends, but Dad was not a traveller – I don't think many West Indians were. If they did go abroad, it would always be back to Jamaica, and they would prepare months in advance, filling large storage barrels with household essentials for family members back home. Mum went to Jamaica when I was fourteen and I hated her going, because I missed her terribly. But I cannot think of anyone who travelled to the West Indies for fewer than four weeks at a time.

But we did have family days out, piling into a coach along with other West Indians and travelling into the countryside where Dad and his teammates would play cricket. Dad loved the game and every Sunday he would get his whites and cricket bat ready and head off to play with the Wadham Lodge cricket club in Walthamstow. I would cringe at the thought of cricket, content to stay at home and watch TV, but I had no choice in the matter. It was the strangest thing: a coachload of Black people and their children driving through a quaint suburban town outside London. After a while we got used to the stares. Much of London was multicultural and, of course, we were used to being around white people. But whenever we travelled outside London for 'away' matches there'd be looks, firstly of shock, and then apprehension as we poured out of the coach. At the time, the West Indian cricket team was one of the best in the world, and you could see the trepidation on the faces of the white opponents as Dad and his teammates greeted them.

But those family days were about so much more than the game. All the mothers would cook chicken and fried fish, and bring West Indian 'hard dough' bread and bake cakes for the occasion, because even though lunch was provided for the team, that provision did not extend to the families. But the kids loved it that way – nothing tasted better than Mum's cooking, and it was even sweeter when it was set up as a picnic. It never mattered that Dad got lunch because he would always help himself to *our food*. Which was never a problem because Mum always made enough for everyone. West Indian parents were strict, but those cricket outings were the one time we were all allowed to roam free. As long as we stayed together, we could go where we liked. The only thing we didn't do was watch cricket. Now and again we would hear Dad shout out, 'Bowled him!', because that was Dad's speciality – he was a master bowler.

Sometimes we would make friends with the local children, but that didn't happen too often. On the way home we would stop off at Dad's social club where the women would sit and chat and the men would play dominoes as if it were a game of poker. 'Yu see what me 'ave now, yu see it, I going to kill yu wid dis move now,' men would shout, before slamming the domino on to the table. I once watched a man run from one side of the room to the other, before he crashed the domino on the table, almost breaking it. By the time we arrived home, we would be shattered. Despite my initial reluctance, I always enjoyed those days out with my family.

Truth be told, it was also a bit of a relief to escape television during those times. We could enjoy being children, running free, enjoying time with our families and community, and not worry about being perceived or cast in a negative light. In 1979, as part of its Open Door Series, which gave community groups access to the airwaves, to talk about their own issues and give their own views, without editorial input, BBC Two broadcast *It Ain't Half Racist, Mum*. The half-hour show was made in association with the Campaign Against Racism in the Media. The programme highlighted the racial slurs present in family sitcoms, and primetime current affairs programmes giving platforms to voices like Enoch Powell as experts in discussions around migration, as well as giving airtime to the then National Front leader, Martin Webster.[85]

The Campaign Against Racism in the Media argued that the media were part of the problem, perpetuating myths and stereotypes about Black people, by omission, distortion or selection, and giving racists inflated importance and respectability.[86]

Sometimes I would catch Dad cursing under his breath as he heard the racist comments on TV. It's unthinkable that they'd be aired now, but back then it was the normal way of things. Racist men would sit in a TV studio speaking about immigration, about *us*, like we did not matter, describing us as a problem and linking us to crime, but there would be no Black people to give their point of view. In 1979 the National Front failed to secure any seats in the election and their leader John Tyndall was replaced by Martin Webster, who decided on 'audacious activity'.

What that meant was the distribution of racist comics to school-children, featuring characters with names like 'Ali the Paki' and 'Sambo'. Webster stated, 'The comics are written in good, honest, straight language for young people, and convey very simple basic ideas of patriotism in a way that's acceptable and appreciated by young people, and as propaganda they're *brilliant*.'[87]

Bulldog was the National Front's youth magazine and was founded in 1977 by sixteen-year-old Joe Pearce, who believed most schools in London's East End were inundated with communist teachers. The magazine encouraged schoolchildren to name and shame them.[88] In 1980, Stephen Harrowell was teaching the history of the Soviet Union, which was part of the syllabus, when two young thugs burst into the classroom and verbally abused him, resulting in an altercation in front of a classroom of students. Harrowell was accused of indoctrinating the minds of young British people with foul communist ideas. Other teachers in Britain had petrol poured through their letterboxes or were beaten up. But such actions failed to bring down the multiracial society. Joe Pearce was jailed in 1982 for incitement of racial hatred.[89]

My family never saw any copies of *Bulldog* or came across a National Front comic, and it's doubtful they would have been distributed in Tottenham. Luckily, we were not subjected to its racist propaganda. But that was the point in my life when the rot began to set in. I was living in a country that took such a pride in its Britishness, but how could I feel part of it when the wheels of racism continued to turn?

THE EDUCATION
—AL
VOID

CHAPTER
X

For the first two years of secondary school, my love of English continued. I was good at languages, getting into the top stream to study German with the chosen few in my year. Mum and Dad would come to all my parents' evenings, where my teachers would discuss what qualifications I would need to become a lawyer, which was my dream. Everything was going exactly as it should, but then everything changed, starting with the first broadcast of *Roots*, and the lack of understanding from teachers that left a growing resentment in me. Importantly, seeing my ancestors in bondage and being treated as less than nothing had a profound effect on how I saw myself. *I felt worthless.* Then there was the Queen's Jubilee, when I saw the whole country celebrating, whilst most of us within the Black community felt like outsiders. And the scariest part of all, I'd wanted to join in, to enjoy the moment, but knew I would not be welcomed.

It all came to a head towards the end of the school year in 1978, when I got to experience first-hand what outcasts we were. It was coming up to my fourteenth birthday, and my classmates and I were on our way home from school. We'd piled on to the top deck of the bus and a white woman, who probably had every right to be upset because all of us were pushing to get on, shoved one of my Black classmates. An argument ensued between them, and, despite the fact that there were white and Black students involved in the row, a man turned to my friend and told her to go back to where she came from. We all started shouting, telling him we were born here and had every right to be here, at which point other white passengers joined in, agreeing with the man. It was awful. We gave as good as we got, but these were adults shouting at children. Yes, we were rowdy and passengers were entitled to give us a ticking off. But in the end, it always came down to our colour. Racism always found a way to rear its ugly head, and with it came an overwhelming feeling of rejection. Why should I have had to justify my right to be here? It made no sense! This country was all I knew. Why was it so hard for them to accept us? We all got off the bus and, like any young people would, we blustered about how they were racists and we'd dealt with them. We were all acting really brave, but as we went our separate ways and I walked home, there was no bravery, just an anger and growing resentment towards people whose racist ideas would not be curbed, even when dealing with children.

In 1965, James Baldwin told Cambridge University, 'It comes as a great shock to discover the country which is your birth-place, and to which you owe your life and your identity, has not in its whole system of reality evolved any place for you.'[90] His words resonated with me. I never mentioned the bus incident to my parents and neither did my friends to theirs, and none of us talked about it to our teachers. Instead, we talked about it amongst ourselves. (I had no idea at the time that in adulthood, I would be hiding in corners or corridors with fellow Black colleagues, talking about racism *among ourselves*.) It was as if we wore two faces: the one we showed our teachers and the one we portrayed to the world outside.

It was like carrying this massive weight on our backs that we tried to drop, but were never allowed to. It would have been great to talk to my parents about what had happened, but it was hard to express your feelings to parents back then. You simply dealt with it; there was no Childline you could ring. But the simple truth is, I didn't deal with it, and it affected me in ways I could not have imagined.

When my grades began to fall, and my confidence took a turn for the worse, I put that down to lacking ability, not being bright enough to succeed. Over the next two years, whilst my white classmates in the top streams excelled, I spiralled in a downward motion that took away any hope of getting the grades I needed for university and becoming a lawyer. I should have been stronger, because my parents had put up with so much to give my sister, brothers and me a better life in this country. I should have had more fight in me. I was bright, I knew I was, but I allowed incidents in my past to hinder my future. I fell by the wayside like so many others, and when I was fifteen and my form teacher told me that I was not A-level material, I believed her; *why wouldn't I?*

Other than my parents, my teachers were key in moulding my ideals. I saw them day in and day out during the most impressionable years of my life. Dad told me not to believe my form teacher. But that bright young promising student was gone, and I was all that was left. How could my form teacher be wrong? I never saw any Black MPs, lawyers, doctors or judges. So my teacher's evaluation of me took hold. I left school at sixteen with no O levels (equivalent to GCSEs today), and went on to a further education college, where I managed to scrape some O levels together in the hope of securing an office job. I could not understand how I started out with so much potential, so much promise, only to fall at the final hurdle, when it counted the most. Was it me? Was it that I simply was not good enough?

In 1974 James Baldwin said that Black American children were victims of the principles on which a country was run, and that 'to get an education in a racist society requires a tremendous act of will.'[91] His words resound like bells with their parallel to the British educational system, highlighting the findings of Bernard Coard in his book first published in 1971 titled, *How the West Indian Child is Made Educationally Subnormal in the British School System*.[92] Coard, a Grenadian who worked in South-east and East London as a teacher and youth worker during the 1960s, found that racism was the main reason why Black children were failing in school. He identified three key factors: low expectations of a Black child's ability within the British educational system, low motivation to succeed academically because Black children feel the cards are stacked against them and low expectations within the Black child in respect of their own abilities, which affect the Black child's image of themselves.

I cannot imagine how frustrating it must have been for a Black teacher like Bernard Coard to work within an educational system that was failing the children it was supposed to protect. What if someone like Coard had been in my school when my grades started to fall? He had an understanding of what Black children were experiencing and, coming from the same background, would have been able to pull a lot of us through. The British educational system failed us because it would not accept that our needs were different, that it's impossible to help a child when you have no knowledge or experience of what they have to face on a daily basis.

We were living in a mainly hostile white environment, with Enoch Powell never far from a TV screen, telling audiences in America that 90 per cent of the British population agreed with what he was saying, and being cheered for it. This was in the mainstream, there for everyone to see. Which would have included our teachers. Yet not one of my white teachers ever asked me how I was feeling about what was going on around me. When my grades started to fall it should have been a red flag that something was wrong, but to them, it felt as if I was just another number. And that hurts.

The worst part of all is that when I started to falter, the teachers blamed it on my ability, and as Coard's template predicted, low expectations of me led me to lose my motivation. Instead of encouraging me, my teachers made it clear that I was not capable of attaining a higher education; that university was

not for me. I went from aspiring to be a lawyer to just *being*...
But I wasn't alone, and just as I was affected, so were many Black
children. In its 1977 report on the West Indian community, the
Commons Select Committee on Race Relations and Immigration
highlighted widespread concerns about the poor performance
of West Indian children in schools, recommending that the
government institute a high-level, independent inquiry into
the causes of this underachievement.[93]

In 1979, my final year at secondary school, Labour Education
Secretary Shirley Williams established the Committee of Inquiry
into the Education of Children from Ethnic Minority Groups.
Led by Anthony Rampton, it aimed to find out why West Indian
children were underperforming at school and to find ways of
putting matters right.

The Committee collated extensive evidence from individuals
and organisations. In addition, a series of open meetings were
arranged with West Indian young people and their parents in the
evenings and at weekends. I wished my parents had been asked,
but they never were. But it's doubtful Dad would have gone – he,
like most of the West Indian community, simply did not trust
the system. Although my start had been promising, none of my
siblings left school with any meaningful qualifications. Besides,
my parents had been living in Britain for over twenty years and
nothing much had changed, so why should the Rampton Report
be any different?

Concern about West Indian children and their performance at
school had been expressed as early as the 1960s. In 1963 a study
by Brent London Education Authority found the performance
of West Indian children was, on average, much lower than that of
white children in reading, arithmetic, and spelling.[94] In 1965,
a study was carried out that compared West Indians in London
and Hertfordshire. It showed similar results.[95] In 1966 and
1968 studies of the reading standards of nine-year-olds in the
Inner London Education Authority showed that West Indian

children at primary school were performing at lower levels than white children from the same socio-economic background. From 1978 to 1979, 9 per cent of West Indians scored higher grades in English compared with 21 per cent of Asians and 29 per cent of other school leavers. In Mathematics, 5 per cent of West Indians scored higher grades compared with 19 per cent of other leavers, and 3 per cent obtained five or more higher grades compared with 18 per cent of Asians and 16 per cent of other leavers.

The Rampton Report found that I was just one of many West Indian children who were underachieving within the British educational system, a matter of grave concern, not only to those involved in education but also, to the whole community. There was evidence establishing that racism had a direct and important bearing on the performance of West Indian children in school. I did not like being a statistic, but that's precisely what I was. I had hoped seeing the figures in black and white would give me some kind of vindication, but it didn't. If anything, it made me feel worse, because clearly there was a problem, and the failure to do anything about it meant that I and those like me had fallen through the cracks of an inept educational system.

There was also widespread opinion among teachers to whom the Committee spoke that West Indian pupils inevitably caused difficulties. These pupils were, therefore, seen either as problems to be put up with or, at best, deserving sympathy. Such negative and patronising attitudes could not lead to a constructive or balanced approach to education. Teacher training, both initial and in-service was required to encourage more positive attitudes towards West Indian children.

Low expectations of the academic ability of West Indian pupils often proved to be self-fulfilling prophecies. As I read the findings, it made me want to turn back time. I wanted to scream aloud, 'If only I had known!' Maybe I would have tried harder to prove to my teachers that they were wrong about me, instead of playing out a part they had written for me, where the only one who came out the loser was me.

Recommendations within Rampton's report included further teacher training in respect of interaction with West Indian children, greater parental involvement for West Indians in their children's education and a recruitment drive for more Black teachers. In all my years at school I never had a Black teacher, and I truly believe it would have made a difference, because the most important aspect of all would have been the example they set. If they could make it in the professional world, I could make it.

Anthony Rampton's interim report was completed on 27 February, 1981, but it was leaked to the press prior to formal publication, which did not take place until 17 June, 1981. On 6 July, 1981, Tom Ellis, MP for Wrexham commented in a debate titled 'West Indian Children' (Rampton Report), that *The Economist* gave positive feedback: 'The whole subject – that is, the poor educational attainment of West Indian children – is embarrassing. To discuss it frankly is useful. To produce an agreed report on it, from an official committee of all races and practically all political views, is a considerable achievement.'[96]

However, he went on to state that other press reactions were scathing of the findings, levelling criticism at the Committee itself – it was hopelessly divided, its meetings were a shambles and Anthony Rampton lacked intellectual bite. The worst of the criticism, however, was aimed at us, the West Indian children, with *The Times* education correspondent stating, '[They] . . . should not have assumed so easily that the low achievement of West Indian pupils necessarily equalled underachievement, as they had gathered no firm statistical evidence to prove that West Indians are in fact performing at a level below their capabilities.'[97]

The Rampton Report's findings that teachers could be directly or indirectly racist was not a popular message and, under pressure from Mark Carlisle, the Education Secretary in Margaret

Thatcher's Conservative government, Anthony Rampton was forced to resign. Rampton was said to have been deeply upset — not by his departure, but by the way *inconvenient truths were being suppressed*.[98] Rampton received no official recognition for his work but 'earned the abiding gratitude of millions of ordinary Black and white men and women and a large number of educationalists'.[99]

The Committee's final report, titled as 'The Swann Report — Education for All', chaired by Lord Swann, was published four years later in 1985.[100] It broadly repeated Rampton's conclusions in relation to the underachievement of Caribbean children as compared to Asian and white children. But the emphasis shifted away from anti-racist strategies towards the provision of support for and acknowledgement of children's different cultural backgrounds within the classroom. Speaking a second language should be seen as a 'positive asset', for instance. It saw multicultural education as enabling 'all ethnic groups, both minority and majority, to participate fully in shaping society . . . whilst also allowing, and where necessary assisting, the ethnic minority communities in maintaining their distinct ethnic identities within a framework of commonly accepted values'.

In embracing multicultural differences, the Swann Report did not address the racism that continued to exist in the perceptions of teachers, in particular with regard to Black boys, and it was hard to see how embracing other cultures would combat the negative stereotypes already formulated in teachers' minds. The report also rejected the notion of separate 'ethnic minority' schools, despite acknowledging the long-standing presence of Anglican, Catholic and Jewish schools.[101] I would describe my secondary school experience as setting off on a journey along with my white peers. We all set off at the same place and were given maps to navigate our way. But it was only when we got to that first fork in the road that I realised our maps were different and I was directed along an alternate route in *the wrong direction*.

My map was presented to me in 1979 at the age of fifteen, when I was told that I was not A-level material.

I am not surprised that the evidence of Rampton's report was not well received, because to admit it was factually correct the government would have had to come to terms with the fact that racism was entrenched within the British educational system directly and indirectly. The problem with not accepting there was a problem, however, was a growing resentment among West Indians of an educational system that had failed them.

THATCHER
—ISM
&
EDUCATION

CHAPTER XI

There is no doubt that education has evolved over the past three decades, but it was Margaret Thatcher's 1988 Education Reform Act that shaped the modern education system that we see today. 'Parents would vote with their children's feet and schools actually gained resources when they gained pupils.'[102]

The Act created an 'education market'; a school effectively became a business, and the chief principle was 'marketisation', based on competition. Parents could choose where to send their children. The National Curriculum introduced a standardised curriculum, where state schools across the country would teach the same subjects and the same content. It saw the creation of Ofsted, the government organisation that inspected schools. Schools would receive funding directly, and the money allocated would depend on the number of students they had. League tables were also introduced, where all school results were published for parents to see.

In 1988 I was twenty-four and had left an educational system that had failed me, but I wanted to feel positive about the education of those Black children who were coming after me in the hope that improvements within the educational system would benefit them. But what Margaret Thatcher's government ignored, as had previous governments, was the fact that Britain was not an equal society. Resources within schools in my borough were limited, and in any market in which competition existed, children in deprived areas would become casualties.

The lack of work opportunities for our parents and the discriminatory way in which we had been educated limited life choices for many of us. People from the Black community were trapped in low-paying jobs, so they were unable to secure places for their children in the more sought-after schools. The new system has led to an improvement in educational standards and, despite changes in governments, the fundamental principles of the 1988 reforms have remained in place. However, the push for excellence within the school system has resulted in a serious knock-on effect for vulnerable pupils, research has found.[103]

Although school took its toll on my confidence and belief in myself, I survived without being excluded. Of course, there were days when I played up in class, but I was always careful not to go too far. Not so much because of my teacher's reaction, but because of that of my parents. In the West Indian community, the worst thing you could do was bring shame on your family, and that would include getting kicked out of school. There was also a rule about hanging around the streets. Dad's words were, 'When school finish, yu come straight home.' But I did not have league tables to contend with, and what could have happened to me if my lack of academic prowess were to bring my school down within the competitive educational world?

In August 2018, a report carried out by *The Times* revealed that Ofsted had expressed concern about the process known as off-rolling,[104] a process in which thousands of badly performing pupils are expelled in the weeks before their GCSEs as state schools look to boost their position in the league tables. More than 30,000 pupils had not had their GCSE results recorded in tables, despite previously appearing on school registers over the past three years. *The Times* also found that 4,175 pupils were put in Pupil Referral Units in the months leading up to exam season in 2018.[105]

A recent study revealed that Black Caribbean pupils were nearly four times more likely to receive a permanent exclusion than the school population as a whole and were twice as likely to receive a fixed-period exclusion. Reasons included teachers' low expectations and institutional racism, lack of diversity in the school workforce, including teachers, and lack of effective training of staff on multicultural education, diversity, and race issues.[106]

But what's also significant is not just how history is repeating itself, but how these young people are perceived by society – a perception even I am guilty of. I would be angered at seeing a group of Black boys hanging around the streets. Why aren't they in school? It wouldn't have entered my mind that a number of them might have been excluded and had nowhere else to go. I never thought about how susceptible they were to being exploited by gang networks. Why? Because I was working hard to get through the system, doing the best I could to survive. It looked to me like they had given up, but of course there must have been a lot more to it than that. So many of them were falling through the cracks, and there is evidence of children being out of the school system for over a year.[107] The difference between one GCSE and no GCSEs is enormous, because it affects life choices, and once pupils are out of mainstream school it is incredibly difficult to get back in. I never had the stigma of being excluded from school, but, if doors were closed for someone like me, how difficult was it for those young people who had been excluded? Even for those who made it back into a mainstream school, how could they overcome the low expectations held by teachers and those within the educational system? I wish I had looked at those boys differently, tried to understand them more.

'FIGHT FOR FAIRNESS'

CHAPTER
XII

In December 2020, the Minister for Women and Equalities, Liz Truss, revealed the Conservatives' new approach to tackling inequality. Dubbed as her 'New Fight for Fairness' speech, she said, 'Too often, the Equality debate has been dominated by a small number of unrepresentative voices, and by those who believe people are defined by their protected characteristic and not by their individual character.'[108]

The current government is moving away from looking at people with protected characteristics facing inequality, which will include those from Black minorities, in order to focus on inequality as a whole. They are gathering evidence through a large-scale Equality Data Programme to better understand the barriers that people from every ethnicity face across the UK. In their new quest, looking at where people are held back, they will consider geographical area as well as social background.[109]

I don't disagree with the government's approach because inequality is wrong, however you look at it. It does not matter whether you are Black, Brown, or white. Everyone has the right to equality, but as I think about the unequal treatment I have faced in my own life and consider the lives of young Black boys excluded from school with little hope of a successful educational future, it's impossible not to feel angered by the government's assumption that there is no difference between the inequality faced by Black people and that faced by White people in Britain. By understanding everyone, the process in relation to how Black people experience inequality is diluted, because when I walk into a room as a Black person, the way I am *perceived* is very different to the way a white person is perceived. When I lead a meeting, or explain a legal issue, in a clear and concise way, it is not uncommon for me to hear comments from my white colleagues as to how 'articulate' I am. Why is my ability to be articulate met with such an element of surprise?

But if inequality is not linked to racism, how can the government explain why it is that inequality still exists for those who have managed to achieve academic excellence? Despite the fact that high proportions of Black people and ethnic minorities are achieving the academic grades needed to obtain a position within the academic world, figures released in 2019–20 show that only 155 out of 23,000 university professors are Black, the fifth year in a row where Black professors have made up less than 1 per cent of total professors in the UK. Can they explain how in the last five years the number of professorships has risen by 3,000, and within that time the number of Black professors has only risen by 55?

What this large-scale governmental project on equality fails to acknowledge is that these people have in fact made it to the other side, achieved their goal of academic excellence, crossed boundaries, irrespective of the disadvantages they faced and the geographical area in which they lived. Yet they are still being held back. Why are these graduates disproportionately represented within the world of academia? What governments over the decades have failed to accept is how racism impacts on people's lives and affects all age groups, from the young to the old.

In 2018, Nottingham Trent University student Rufaro Chisango locked herself in her room and posted video footage of fellow students chanting 'We hate the Blacks' outside her door, and a stream of other racist abuse.[110] Another student from the same university, Amrik Singh, was forced to leave a bar in nearby Mansfield simply for wearing a turban.[111] A Bournemouth University student, Telma Rodrigues, uncovered racist comments being made about her by former school classmates in a group chat, in which she was described as a 'big Black ape', a 'cotton-picking f—' and 'gorilla-looking motherf—'.[112] At Warwick University, another Black student, Faramade Ifaturoti, found the words 'monkey' and 'nigga' written on the skin of bananas.[113] And a student at De Montfort University in Leicester complained about being repeatedly called a nigger by her fellow students, who also sang to her about lynching.[114]

On 17 January, 2020 on *BBC Question Time*, Actor Laurence Fox was greeted by rapturous applause after saying, 'We are the most tolerant, lovely country . . . It's so easy to throw the charge of racism at everybody and it's really starting to get boring now.'[115]

One of the biggest hurdles for those facing racism is the attitude of people within our society who are unwilling to accept how seriously it can affect a person's life because they have never experienced it. Laurence Fox was educated at the prestigious public school, Harrow and, despite being expelled from the school before his A levels, has managed to carve a successful career as an actor. To Fox, racism may be 'boring', but he can only say that because he has never been directly affected by it.

In 2020 Truss stated, 'Britain is one of the best places in the world to live, no matter your skin colour, sexuality, religion or anything else. We need to be positively empowering people in Britain to succeed so everyone has access to opportunity, not using positive discrimination.'

It is difficult to see how Liz Truss's 'New Fight for Fairness' is not flawed when it fails to incorporate the crucial fact that racism is a significant factor within the unfairness faced by the Black community, and this applies whether they have studied to degree level, or been excluded from school, with no qualifications whatsoever.

BURNING AN ILLUSION & MY WALK OF SHAME

CHAPTER
XIII

It was 1980, my sixteenth year, when my sister Anne arrived from Jamaica to live with us in our house in Tottenham. Mum and Dad had wanted her to come a lot sooner, but my grandmother did not want to let her go. But as she grew older, my parents were determined to bring her to Britain to live with us. Joyce was seventeen, Glen was ten and Fitz twelve. It wasn't an easy transition for anyone, with a strange older sister suddenly descending upon us. It must have been a lot harder for Anne, because she was leaving everything she knew, and I cannot imagine the wrench it must have been for her to leave our grandmother, a woman I had never met, but the only mother Anne had known.

Joyce and I first wondered where Anne was going to sleep. The two of us were already sharing a room, but Dad set up an extra bed that could be folded away during the day. It took Anne a while to settle in, but within a few months she got a job with Mum as a machinist. Anne was not afraid of hard work, and with her wages she was able to buy the things she wanted without having to rely on our parents. She had the same strength and resilience our parents had had when they first came to the UK, but thankfully, by the time she arrived in Britain, skinheads and racist signs were few and far between. Besides, we lived in Tottenham, which had a large Black community; it was unlikely any racist would have dared attempt to try anything, because if they did they would have regretted it.

It was also the year I finally received my National Insurance number. But I have to admit, with some embarrassment, I was a little bland. I didn't stand out in a crowd, I wasn't pretty, there was nothing special about me and I preferred my own company. So, I locked myself away in my room where I would listen to bands like The Specials, UB40 or The Beat, or immerse myself in a book. It was easier that way because I was a little inept socially. I didn't feel comfortable around young people my age and never really fitted in. Still, I was determined to carve a future for myself, make something of my life. After leaving school with virtually no qualifications, I enrolled at the North London College of Further Education, in the hope of gaining the O levels I needed. I knew I wouldn't stand any chance without them.

But that year was also to show me how, with strength and fortitude, it was possible to change your life. Mum suffered badly from asthma and her condition was made worse by the dust she had to put up with working as a machinist. There were several long admissions to hospital. One day she called me into her room and told me that a friend had let her know about a domestic job at the Royal Free Hospital. She asked me to help her fill out the application form. We went through the questions one by one, name, address, and so on. When we got to 'education', I asked Mum what she wanted me to put. She said, 'Just put general education, but that I am prepared to work hard.'

Mum could read and write, but she lacked the confidence to put her words down on paper, so I was happy to do it. She secured an interview and got the job. The elation I felt was amazing. Although to some a domestic service role may not exactly be considered 'high-flying', for Mum it meant escaping dust-filled rooms and sewing machines. Most importantly, working for the NHS gave her a fair wage, a pension, annual leave and sick pay. It was just the start for Mum, as she would go on to bigger and better things. She could have continued as a machinist, but she made a decision to change her life. *If only I were that brave.*

Joyce and I could not have been more different. While I beavered away at college, she landed an administrative job in an office in Shoreditch and brought home a good wage. She also had day release from work to study, and took on a business course. Her job enabled her to keep up with the casual fashions of the day: pristine cotton blouses or dresses trimmed with lace, low-heeled shoes and her hair pressed and neatly curled. Boys would sport Afros and wear jumpers and slick trousers and shoes.

When she wasn't working, Joyce immersed herself in the world of lovers rock, listening to the likes of Janet Kay, Sandra Cross, Carroll Thompson and Jean Adebambo to name but a few. I loved it when she was at work and I had a day off college, because I would dress up in her lace tops and play her records on my small portable record player. She'd have killed me if she knew, but luckily for me she never found out.

The iconic film *Burning an Illusion* directed by Menelik Shabazz's first feature, released in 1981, took us to Notting Hill and Ladbroke Grove, where we saw Black young voices come alive on the big screen. In Thatcher's London, unemployment was high in Britain, and the Black community were disproportionately affected. This film showed how a young Black couple coped with that, alongside the racism that existed within the police, and it was told through the eyes of someone like me. It was uplifting to see how a black woman fought against racism to reach a place of cultural self-awareness. The film won the Grand Prix at the Amiens International Film Festival, with actor Cassie McFarlane winning the Evening Standard Most Promising Newcomer Award.[116]

My generation were fighting for an identity not knowing where we fitted in, and films like *Burning an Illusion* broke away from the system incorporated within Thatcherism and showed us a new consciousness. But even though the message was a powerful one, we as a generation had no power. But we had a belief in ourselves – we were better than the negative stereotypes plastered across the media.

For those of us lucky enough to travel to what Enoch Powell defined as our country of origin, while there we stood out, with names such as 'foreigner' or 'English girl' being thrown in our direction by native Jamaicans who saw us as outsiders. Our English accents only emphasised the differences between us and our cousins. For some reason, they had this mythical idea that in Britain life was sweet and we wanted for nothing. Economically, Britain was more affluent, but our cousins had no understanding of the barriers that existed, of how hard it was to be accepted. For us, it was wonderful to meet our Jamaican families, but the differences between us could not be ignored. As for Britain, it was a place where a lot of us felt like guests who had outstayed their welcome.

Whilst at college I wasn't sure what I wanted, but I figured if I couldn't get to university and become a lawyer, I would find a job with career prospects. A few streets away from my college, there was an Army recruitment office, and one day a white college friend and I decided to go and find out about a career in the Army. As far as I knew, the Army offered opportunities as well as the chance to travel, which I wanted to explore. Two recruitment officers dressed in uniform were at the front desk. They stared at us as we walked in. I immediately knew something was wrong, because I saw the way they looked at my white friend and then at me. We explained why we were there. They both smiled, watching her attentively. It was hard, going through the embarrassment of standing there as they both fumbled around, working out who would draw the short straw and get me. It was clear that neither of them wanted the task. Finally, one officer walked over to my friend and said, 'I'll deal with you.' The other officer looked at me blankly and showed me into a room, where he asked me to sit down.

The next few minutes were some of the most agonising of my

life. I sat there in front of this officer, who was totally detached in finding out who I was or what my interests were. He just pulled out a leaflet and went through it. It took less than five minutes, after which we simply sat in silence. I wanted to run out, but didn't have the courage, aware that my friend was still in the other room. I could hear there was an animated conversation going on. You'd think things could not get much worse, but after a while this officer looked at me and said he was not allowed to leave, so would I mind going to the shops and buying him a packet of cigarettes?

I stood up and agreed to go. He fiddled in his pocket, gave me the money and I obediently nipped to the shop on the corner and returned just in time to see my friend leaving the room. I gave him the cigarettes and his change, and we left.

On our way back to college, my friend told me all about the information she'd been given. I cannot remember any of it, because I was still trying to take in what had happened to me. I didn't join the Army. The woman I am today would have gone to the shops, bought the cigarettes and promptly returned to ram them down his throat. I call that trip to the newsagent's my *walk of shame*, because each time I think of it, I feel humiliation and regret.

Like most bad incidents in my life, I put it to the back of my mind, stored it away in a file of unpleasant memories. I felt worthless that day. Of course, I could not have been more wrong. But that experience was just another that chipped away at my confidence. Unless you go through it yourself, it's impossible to understand how being treated like that makes you feel. With all your power, you want to brush the memory away, move on, but the feeling stays with you, even though you've done nothing wrong. I felt it was so unfair that my young life had already been filled with so much disappointment. It seemed like everything I wanted, or dared to even try was scuppered by this horrible word, 'racism'. But at the same time, I didn't want it to beat me. I wanted to overcome it, to be strong enough to succeed in spite of it. I didn't want to be a failure, and I would have been if I'd hung on to feelings of resentment and anger. But it was what I was going through, along with the rest of my generation and no one more so than our young Black men, who in 1981 erupted and became part of history in the making as the streets of Brixton lit up.

1981, THE SUMMER OF ERUPTION

CHAPTER
XIV

The most difficult obstacle the Black community had to face following the summer riots of 1981 was the violence against the police seen on TV, because the danger with any violent response to injustice is that the reasons for the disturbance become lost. The white community saw the bloodied faces of officers who became heroes, taking on the might of an aggressive, lawless community. But as my family and I watched the events on our television, it was like walking into a play halfway through and not being privy to important elements of the plot that took place earlier on. At the end of the play, you might still draw the same conclusions, but you are not fully informed of the facts.

There is no doubt that there were serious problems in Brixton at the time, with the rate of muggings going up four times faster than in any other London borough.[117] In 1980 the number of crimes recorded in the Borough of Lambeth was 30,805. The Brixton Division was responsible for 10,626 of those crimes. Between 1976 and 1980, Brixton accounted for 35 per cent of all crimes in the borough, but 49 per cent of all robbery and violent theft offences.[118] This was the reasoning behind Swamp 81, an undercover operation launched by Commander Brian Fairbairn involving ten squads of plain-clothed police officers who were given the remit of stopping and searching any Black man that happened to move around the central Brixton area. In just five days, 943 people were stopped and searched, and 82 arrested, through the heavy use of what was colloquially known as the 'sus law'. The difficulty the Black community faced was that a lot of innocent people were being caught in the net, victimised for no other reason than being Black.

Linking the disturbances in 1981 to people merely being Black was also a key feature of an interview in which Enoch Powell made it clear that he was of the opinion social issues were not a relevant factor, stating, 'Social conditions have nothing to do with it because the same social conditions do not produce those consequences where the Alien Wedge is not present.' [119]

Eldon Griffiths MP also commented, 'Violence cannot be explained away by social factors. In the '30s we had far worse housing, far fewer social services, but people didn't go mad and start throwing Molotov cocktails about.'[120]

Despite recriminations on the part of Enoch Powell and those with similar views, the discontent stirred the Conservative government into action, with Home Secretary William Whitelaw appointing Lord Scarman to inquire urgently into the 1981 Brixton riots. The inquiry highlighted the concern of the Black community about the tragic deaths in New Cross of thirteen young Black people aged between fourteen and twenty-two, who attended a birthday party and were killed in a mysterious fire that eyewitnesses attested was caused by a petrol bomb.[121] The subsequent police investigation failed to uncover the truth behind the deaths, and there was an insensitive reaction from the press. The report revealed that over 12,000 dwellings in the Borough of Lambeth were defined by the local authority as unfit, and a further 8,250 lacked one or more basic amenity. Some 20 per cent of the total housing stock was therefore substandard, and a further 12 per cent was in need of major renovation. The report also found that most of the worst housing was in Brixton.[122]

Over the year up to February 1981, total unemployment in Great Britain increased by nearly 66 per cent, compared with 82 per cent for ethnic minorities alone. The report found that without doubt Blacks were over-represented among the registered and unregistered young unemployed.[123] In the Brixton Employment Office, the rate of registered unemployed among Black males under nineteen was estimated at 55 per cent.[124]

The Scarman Report also looked at police accountability, stating, 'Accountability is the constitutional mechanism which can provide the backing: for it renders the police answerable for what they do.'[125] It recognised the error of judgement that could be applied to the senior officers responsible for authorising such an intrusive police operation as Swamp 81 without proper consultation with the community, and the police's failure to take into account that some of the executing officers were racially prejudiced towards Black people on the street.

Significantly, the report also pointed out that it may have been only too easy for some officers, faced with what they saw as the relentless rising tide of street crime, to slip into the mindset that all young Black people were potential criminals, when in fact, like white criminals in relation to the total white population, a very small proportion of the Black population committed crime. Bringing the community on board, listening to their concerns and working with them might have led to a peaceful outcome without the eruption of rioting. Although Brixton provided the focus for the inquiry, Lord Scarman emphasised that he would look at Brixton in a national context, given the serious disorders that also occurred in July 1981, in London's Southall, Liverpool's Toxteth, the Moss Side area of Manchester, Handsworth, Wolverhampton, Smethwick, the centre of Birmingham and the West Midlands.

The troubles in Southall, home to a large Asian community, began when a large group of white skinhead youths, mainly from the East End of London, who were on their way to attend a concert in a public house, began smashing shop windows in The Broadway. This led to a battle between Asian people and skinheads and, when the police got in their way, the Asians then attacked the police. Southall differed from Brixton in that it didn't suffer from a high rate of street crime, but the inquiry found that Southall was a pocket within the affluent area of West London that suffered deprivation, with high levels of unemployment, particularly among its ethnic minority population.

Unlike the West Indian community, aggrieved by alleged harassment at the hands of the police, the Asian community felt that the police did not do enough to protect them against racist attacks. Extreme right-wing groups would carry out marches within heavily populated Asian areas, and seeing the police walking alongside these groups gave Asians the impression that the police were somehow in agreement with their views.

The Black community in Liverpool is long established, with some Black Liverpudlians being able to trace their roots in the area over as many as ten generations. This could be linked to Liverpool having been a major port for the transatlantic slave trade, whereas the West Indians settled around inner-city London could be considered the 'new' immigrants. However, many of the issues found in Brixton were equally applicable to Toxteth, Moss Side and the West Midlands, Handsworth, Wolverhampton, Smethwick and the centre of Birmingham: high unemployment, social deprivation, bad housing, high crime rates and heavy policing.

The recommendations made by the Scarman Report were extremely important to the Black community because they provided the government with a blueprint for stemming the *racial disadvantage* that Black people were experiencing through a series of recommendations. These proposed that police should develop formal arrangements in every police force area for consultation between police and community at different levels, and for the involvement of chief officers of police in local social and economic decisions effecting policing. Similarly, there was a need for regular and systematic consultation at borough level in the Metropolitan Police district. More training should be put into place with a new emphasis on the problems of policing a multiracial society, and on the prevention and handling of disorder. The training should apply, not only to new recruits but also, to those in service, especially in the area of supervision and management. The complaints procedure against the police must be substantially reformed to improve public confidence, and there should be an increase in numbers of police officers from ethnic minorities, so that officers better reflected the community in which they worked.[126]

Positive steps were needed to deal with the special needs of ethnic minorities where they existed in education, employment and housing. More support, including private financial and advisory support, should be given to ethnic minority businesses. As well as putting ethnic monitoring in place in order to measure more accurately the extent of the problem, urban programmes should be provided to improve poor housing conditions for the inner city as a whole. The report also recognised the findings of the Interim Report of the Rampton Committee, acknowledging the evidence produced within it by making the point that a significant number of West Indian children had failed to benefit from the British educational system. Lord Scarman stated, 'I do urge speedy action if we are to avoid the perpetuation in this country of an economically dispossessed Black population. A weakness in British society is that there are too few people of West Indian origin in the business, entrepreneurial and professional class.'[127]

Lord Scarman was in a unique position because the inquiry had collated evidence directly from members of the Black community as well as the police, along with gathering extensive information from employment, housing and educational sources. The recommendations made were based upon those findings. I was at college at the time and read the report with interest, but I also realised that, for its recommendations to succeed, innovative and flexible minds were needed, and I was concerned that the administrators required to put things in place would lack the necessary adaptability.

The Scarman Report illustrated that the 1981 summer of discontent was about more than just the tempestuous relationship the Black community had with the police. Irrespective of how difficult the relationship was, the police were not responsible for the social conditions that existed; this responsibility lay squarely at the door of the government. But, just as teachers held the opinion that West Indian pupils inevitably caused difficulties and were problems to be put up with, so the police considered that young Black males, innocent or not, had a propensity to commit more crime than their white counterparts.

Despite my misgivings, I decided to make a life-changing decision. I considered the Scarman recommendations, and thought: if we as a community want change, we should take the initiative to help make that happen. That's when I decided to join the police force. At first, I kept it to myself and didn't tell anyone until I read the recruitment requirements – an entrance test made up of a written paper and a fitness test. I filled out the application and would run to the park every morning to build up my fitness.

When I broke the news to my parents, Mum was worried for my safety and I had never seen Dad so upset – he even threatened to disown me if I joined. My siblings were also unhappy, worried about the repercussions for our family. But I made it clear that we couldn't do anything from the outside; if more of us joined then it was bound to make a difference to our community. I was determined not to let the Army recruitment incident affect my judgement – that was then, and this was now, I told myself.

The fateful day arrived, and I entered the exam room to take the test. By then I had secured some O levels and, coming up to my eighteenth birthday, I was studying for A levels. I was on a mission, determined to get through. When the results of the recruitment exam landed on my doormat a few weeks later I opened the envelope in anticipation.

I didn't pass.

I was shattered by the news and I almost sank into a depression. Of course, my family were extremely pleased, but it knocked the stuffing out of me. It was as if the police were paying lip service to the recruitment of Black people, creating tests in which you were pitched against your white counterparts. I never got any feedback from the assessors; it was just a straight *No*. It would have been easy for me to feel hate at that moment, become consumed with resentment, but as the weeks and months went by, I realised that maybe it was not such a bad thing that I did not get in. I needed my family; they were all I had, and to ostracise myself, become part of an organisation that my community didn't trust, might have done them more harm than good. And *what would it have done to me?*

PC
BLAKELOCK
&
POLICE
RETRI
—BUTION

CHAPTER XV

It was 1984, I was in my twenty-first year, and I had moved out of my parents' house and into a flat just off of Philip Lane in Tottenham. It was not the nicest of places, but Dad and I were not getting on, and like any young person I wanted to be free of the rules that came with living with parents. When I saw that there was a flat to rent close to my parents' home, I snapped it up. Fitz and Glen were still at home, and, Joyce, who had married at the end of summer 1981, was living in a lovely two-bedroom flat in Hackney.

Anne, who had also found love, had moved in with her boyfriend. When it came to men in my life, I had boyfriends, but nothing developed into anything too serious, and I liked it that way.

Margaret Thatcher was serving her second term as Prime Minister, and my parents continued to work hard. Leaving home did not stop me from going back on a regular basis for Sunday dinner, or any dinner for that matter, because independent or not, there was nothing like Mum's home cooking.

I visited my sisters regularly, and had built up a circle of close friends from work. I was an admin assistant for the Department of Health and Social Security (now the Department for Work and Pensions).

On the night of Sunday 6 October, 1985, I was asleep in my flat in Tottenham, close to the Broadwater Farm Estate. I was annoyed at being woken up by helicopters throughout the night, and when I looked out the window the sky was red. I had no idea what was happening just a couple of miles away. I had heard about a woman dying after a police search, but for me that was as far as it went. I had lots of friends, an office job and was getting on with living, keeping my head down and staying away from trouble.

But that morning when I left the house and walked on to Philip Lane, everything felt different. There was no damage or carnage anywhere, but there were police officers at the end of each street. There was a feeling of coldness, emptiness in the atmosphere, not just because it was a crisp October morning. An uneasiness. I passed a police officer standing on a corner. He looked at me, I looked back; we smiled at each other, and I went on my way.

It was only when I arrived at work that my colleagues told me what had happened. On Broadwater Farm, just a couple of miles away from where I'd been sleeping, a police officer by the name of PC Keith Blakelock had been killed by rioters. I felt sick at the thought of the violence. Nothing justified what happened to that officer . . . *nothing*. No anger, frustration, bitterness or resentment could justify it, because from the moment they took his life, those murderers became the same as any officer responsible for killing one of us.

But there was something else, an awful dread, as we all wondered – *what were the police going to do about the death of one of their own?* I knew from the way the police had used their tactics before that no one in Tottenham would be safe. I was frightened for my brothers and their friends, and I was right to be so. With the media baying for blood, intense pressure was placed on detectives to solve the case. One hundred and fifty officers were assigned to the case full time, and the inquiry, headed by Detective Chief Superintendent Graham Melvin of the Serious Crime Squad, became the largest in the history of the Metropolitan Police. With vast numbers of police everywhere, it was like living in an occupied zone.

On one hand, I felt sorrow for the death of an officer, and on the other, the fear that I felt for my brothers and their friends, being Black men on the streets, was overwhelming. Dad was extremely nervous – all our parents were – but as a family we never spoke that much about what had happened. There was no chorus of anger at seeing Blakelock's death as some kind of retribution. How could there be? A man had died. But from that moment on, Tottenham would always be associated with the death of a police officer, and the best thing the Black community could do was to keep their heads down.

A total of 359 people were arrested in connection with the inquiry in 1985 and 1986, and only 94 of them were interviewed in the presence of a lawyer. Many of the confessions that resulted, whether directly about the murder, or about having taken part in the rioting, were made before the lawyer was given access to the interviewee.[128]

One resident told the 1986 Gifford Inquiry into the rioting, 'You would go to bed and you would just lie there, and you would think, are they going to come and kick my door, what's going to happen to my children? . . . It was that horrible fear that you lived with day by day, knowing they could come and kick down your door and hold you for hours.' The inquiry heard that 9,165 police officers were either deployed on the estate or held in reserve between 10 and 14 October, 1985.[129] The police did not hold back pursuit of those they believed responsible. Mark Pennant, aged fifteen, who was diagnosed with learning difficulties and attended a special school, was arrested on 9 October, 1985, and interviewed six times over the course of two days with a teacher in attendance. His mother was not told that he had been taken into custody. When charged with the murder, he asked the teacher who accompanied him, 'Does that mean I have to go and live with you?'[130]

Jason Hill, a thirteen-year-old white boy who lived on Broadwater Farm, was arrested on 13 October, 1985 and held for three days without access to a lawyer. He was kept in a very hot cell, which he said made sleeping and even breathing difficult. His clothes and shoes were removed for forensic tests, and he was interviewed wearing only underpants and a blanket, which was stained with his own vomit by the third day of his detention. Hyacinth Moody of the Haringey Community Relations Council sat in as an 'appropriate adult'; she was criticised by the judge for having failed to intervene.[131] Hill claimed the police had threatened to keep him in the station for two weeks and said he would never see his family again. 'They could have told me [the murderer] was Prince Charles, and I would have said it was him,' said Hill.[132]

Mark Lambie, aged fourteen, was the third minor to be charged with the murder. He was named by Mark Pennant and Jason Hill and interviewed with his father and a solicitor present. Lambie admitted to having taken part in the rioting but denied involvement in the murder. One witness said during the trial that he had seen Lambie force his way through the crowd to reach Blakelock, although the testimony was discredited; the witness was caught in several lies and admitted he had offered evidence only to avoid a prison sentence.[133]

Winston Silcott was twenty-six years old when he was arrested – the eldest of a total of six charged with the murder. Silcott had a chequered past, having been convicted on nine counts of burglary and sent to the youth detention centre, Borstal, for a few months. In 1979 he was sentenced to a further six months for wounding.[134] In September 1980, he stood trial for the murder of nineteen-year-old Lennie McIntosh, a postal worker who had been stabbed and killed at a party in Muswell Hill in 1979.[135] The first trial resulted in a hung jury; a second trial saw him acquitted.[136] In December 1984, Silcott was arrested for the murder of a twenty-two-year-old boxer, Anthony Smith, at a party in Hackney. Silcott was convicted of Smith's murder in February 1986, while awaiting trial for the Blakelock murder, and was sentenced to life imprisonment.[137]

Silcott was arrested for Blakelock's murder on 12 October, 1985, six days after the riot. He was interviewed five times over the course of twenty-four hours. Detective Chief Superintendent Melvin asked the questions and Detective Inspector Maxwell Dingle took the notes. During the first four interviews, Silcott stayed mostly silent and refused to sign the detectives' notes, but during the fifth interview on 13 October, when Melvin said he knew Silcott had struck Blakelock with a machete or sword, his demeanour changed, according to the notes.[138]

Nineteen-year-old Engin Raghip, of Turkish-Cypriot descent, was arrested on 24 October, 1985 after a friend mentioned his name to the police – the only time anyone had linked him to the murder.[139] During his trial, the court heard from an expert that Raghip was 'in the middle of the mildly mentally handicapped range', although this testimony was withheld from the jury.[140] He was held for two days without representation, first speaking to a solicitor on the third day, who said he had found Raghip distressed and disorientated.[141] He was interviewed ten times over a period of four days. He was released on bail, then charged with murder six weeks later, in December 1985, under the doctrine of common purpose, a legal term that makes someone responsible for being one of a group taking part in an illegal enterprise, which in this case was the riot.[142]

Aged eighteen when Blakelock was killed, Mark Braithwaite was a rapper and disc jockey living with his parents in Islington, London. On 16 January, 1986, three months after the murder, his name was mentioned for the first time to detectives by a man they had arrested, Bernard Kinghorn. Kinghorn told them he had seen Braithwaite, whom he said he knew only by sight, stab Blakelock with a kitchen knife. Kinghorn later withdrew the allegation, telling the BBC three years later that it had been false.[143] Braithwaite was held for three days and was at first denied access to a lawyer, on the instruction of DCS Melvin. He was interviewed eight times over the first two days and, with a lawyer present, four times on the third.[144] During the first thirty hours of his detention he had nothing to eat, and said in court, as did several other suspects, that the heat in the cells was oppressive, making it difficult to breathe. In a seventh interview, he said he had hit a police officer, but that it was not Blakelock. On the basis of this confession evidence, he was charged with murder.[145]

Forty-nine men and youths were convicted of offences arising from the riots, out of 359 arrested and 159 charged, not counting the six murder defendants.[146] The trial of the six – the adults Silcott, Raghip and Braithwaite, and the youths Pennant, Hill and Lambie – began in Court Number Two of the Old Bailey on 19 January, 1987.[147] All the men were charged with murder, riot and affray; Lambie was also charged with throwing petrol bombs. The press coverage of the trial included the publication of a notorious close-up of a half-smiling Silcott by the *Sun* on day two, one that 'created a monster to stalk the nightmares of Middle England', as journalist Kurt Barling put it.[148] Silcott said he had been asleep in a police cell when it was taken; he said he was woken up, held in a corridor with his arms pinned against a wall and photographed, and that the expression on his face was one of fear.[149] Its publication constituted 'the most gross contempt', according to the trial judge, Sir Derek Hodgson, yet, no action was taken against the newspaper.[150]

The judge dismissed the charges against the youths because they had been detained without access to parents or a lawyer; in the absence of the jury, the judge was highly critical of the police on that point.[151] Four armoured police vehicles waited in Tottenham as the jury deliberated for three days.[152] They returned on 19 March, 1987 with a unanimous guilty verdict against Silcott, Raghip and Braithwaite; the men were sentenced to life imprisonment, with a recommendation that Silcott serve at least thirty years.[153] One Black female juror fainted when the verdicts were read out. The tabloids knew no restraint, writing about the 'beasts of Broadwater Farm', 'hooded animals', and 'packs of savages', with the old jail-cell image of Silcott published above captions such as 'smile of evil'.[154]

After the three were convicted it was difficult to say how we were feeling within the Black community . . . stunned, dismayed. PC Blakelock had been brutally murdered that night and the police didn't stop until they got their pound of flesh, and right and wrong did not come into it. Rules were broken, and press headlines and photographs obtained illegally incited hatred for an already damaged community, in which the innocent suffered alongside the guilty.[155]

In 1991 the Court of Appeal overturned all three convictions, but a second criminal inquiry began in 1992, led by Commander Perry Nove, who appealed for help from the local Black community. By the end of 1993, Nove had identified nine suspects against whom at least two eyewitnesses would testify, supported by evidence such as photographs.[156] The suspect list included Nicholas Jacobs, who in 2014 would be tried for Blakelock's murder, based on statements gathered during the Nove investigation, and acquitted by jury after trial in April 2014. It transpired during Jacobs's trial that two of the witnesses who testified against him had been paid expenses to the tune of thousands of pounds during Nove's inquiry.[157]

In July 1992 DCS Melvin, who had conducted the first investigation, was charged with perjury and conspiracy to pervert the course of justice, and Dingle with conspiracy.[158] The prosecution alleged that the detectives' notes of the fifth interview with Silcott had been altered after the fact to include several self-incriminating remarks. Silcott had refused to answer questions during the first four interviews.[159] During the fifth interview, when told there were witness statements that he had struck Blakelock with a machete or similar, the notes show Silcott saying, 'Those kids will never go to court. You wait and see. No one else will talk to you. You can't keep me away from them.' Silcott denied ever having said those words.

The detectives were acquitted on 26 July, 1994, by a unanimous verdict.[160] Both had been suspended during the case. Dingle retired immediately. Melvin was greeted as a hero when he returned to work,[161] but he retired three months later.[162]

There was no coming back for the Black community in Tottenham and their relationship with the police after PC Blakelock's death. Even if some of us wished to find a way forward, it was unlikely to succeed, particularly bearing in mind the heavy-handed manner in which the police had conducted the investigation into Blakelock's murder. And then there were the police themselves – I didn't think they would ever be able to move on from his death, and the riots only increased the feelings of distrust on both sides, as if there could never be a mutual respect even at the most basic level. The lines between the Black community and the police had been clearly drawn.

What would have happened if I had been successful in my application and joined the police? Would I have been placed on the front line at Broadwater Farm during the riots, and would I have been made to patrol the streets of Tottenham in their aftermath?

I'm glad I never had to find out.

THE
INFAMOUS
MEMO

CHAPTER
XVI

Every year confidential government documents from twenty years ago are released by the National Archives. The vast majority are typically dull government letters and statements sent between departments, but a few reveal the private attitudes of those in power. In 2015 a five-page memo written to Prime Minister Margaret Thatcher in 1985 was uncovered in which adviser Oliver Letwin and fellow Tory aide adviser Vernon Hartley Booth gave recommendations as to how to respond to the social unrest and rioting in inner-city Black communities.

Letwin and Booth dismissed proposals by two government ministers to invest in a scheme designed to encourage Black entrepreneurs, suggesting that such an initiative would only lead to them spending the money on 'discos and drugs'. The memo said, '[Lord] Young's new entrepreneurs will set up in the disco and drug trade; Kenneth Baker's refurbished council blocks will decay through vandalism combined with neglect; and people will graduate from temporary training or employment programmes into unemployment or crime.'[163] The memo also criticised plans to spend heavily to improve public services and facilities in neighbourhoods hit by riots, comparing the Black communities with generations of white working-class people who they claimed had lived in similar areas without rioting, stating, 'Lower-class, unemployed white people lived for years in appalling slums without a breakdown of public order on anything like the present scale; in the midst of the depression, people in Brixton went out, leaving their grocery money in a bag at the front door, and expecting to see groceries there when they got back.'[164] Letwin and Booth dismissed suggestions that the rioting had been caused by racism or social deprivation, despite evidence that racism in the Metropolitan Police was rampant. 'The root of social malaise is not poor housing, or youth "alienation", or the lack of a middle class,' they wrote.[165]

The pair categorically rejected the idea that the Prime Minister should pursue positive-action initiatives to help close the racial inequality gap and cut the disproportionally large unemployment rate in Black communities. The memo concluded with the words, 'There should be no "positive discrimination" in any new programmes', and also advised Mrs Thatcher to bar her ministers from proposing any state-funded solutions.

After the documents were released in 2015, Mr Letwin 'apologised unreservedly' and admitted parts of the private memo were 'badly worded and wrong'.[166] During his thirty years in politics Letwin had an illustrious career and had influence with Prime Ministers Margaret Thatcher and later David Cameron. In 1987, despite knowing Letwin's views regarding the Black community, the Conservatives endorsed him as the candidate for the Hackney North and Stoke Newington seat – an area with a large Black population. During the election campaign Letwin claimed that Labour candidate Diane Abbott could not represent 'ordinary voters'.[167] He was unsuccessful, with Abbott becoming the first female Black MP in Britain. But what is significant is that, despite Letwin's stigmatisation of the Black community, he remained in an influential role within the corridors of power.

'COME FLY WITH ME'

CHAPTER
XVII

The year 1987 was to end on a high note, with the historic election to the House of Commons of four ethnic minority Members of Parliament: Diane Abbott for Hackney North and Stoke Newington, Paul Boateng for Brent South, Bernie Grant for Tottenham, and Keith Vaz, Britain's longest-serving Asian MP, for Leicester East. This was an important step for the Black community – it meant that Black people now had a direct voice in Parliament for the first time.[168] As a Tottenham resident I was proud that Bernie Grant represented our community, and when he arrived on his first day in Parliament, adorned in traditional African robes, he left no room for doubt that he would be a voice to be reckoned with. Grant held his seat from 1987 until his death in 2000, after which he was replaced by David Lammy who, as I write in 2021, still holds the Tottenham seat today.

I was excited that this had happened. Yes, these were small steps, but, importantly, it was a start. There were some who argued that it was too little too late. Dad was of the opinion the establishment would never change, and that, even if they let a few of us in, this alone would not be enough to repair the damage. But I refused to think that way. Longing for a change in my life, I believed that if they could do it, then *so could I*.

I was a single twenty-three-year-old with no ties. I was determined to break free from the mundane nine-to-five office job. I saw a post advertised for an air stewardess on long-haul flights. Some of my friends told me I could do better and that I'd be nothing more than a glorified waitress, but I figured I would get to travel, something I had always wanted. My application form was pristine. I had a photograph professionally taken to make sure I looked my best and I was extremely excited when I landed an interview with one major airline.

When the day arrived, I dressed to impress, took the train to Gatwick Airport, and joined the other eleven candidates in the room. As expected, the interviewer was dressed immaculately in the airline uniform and was, of course, confident and pleasant. She told us we were the pick of the crop and congratulated us on getting through to the final stages. She asked each of us in turn to say a little bit about ourselves. When my turn came, I spoke about how I had always dreamed of travelling the world, meeting new people, that sort of thing. Although it was a bog-standard answer, I felt I had done pretty well. The woman turned to me and smiled and, as the only Black person in the room, I was ready for anything – that is, anything but her response. 'So,' she said, 'why haven't you applied to a Caribbean airline?'

Her question stopped me dead in my tracks. Had I just arrived in a parallel universe? My application stated 'British', my passport stated 'British'. Even if I'd wanted to apply to a Caribbean airline, I would not have met the criteria, on the basis that *I was British*! I said to her I was born in Britain and as such it only stood to reason that I would apply to a British airline. She nodded and smiled in all the right places, but in that moment I was transported back to that Army recruitment room, only this time I had the other white candidates gawping at me as I tried to justify my presence. Although I was not in any doubt that I would be unsuccessful, it did not stop me from being extremely disappointed when the letter of rejection arrived. That experience taught me yet again that I might see myself as one thing, but other people, those who made the rules, saw me as something else.

Looking back, I realise I had committed the worst crime of all as I did not report that airline employee, and there was no excuse. At least when I walked out of the Army recruitment office, I had the excuse of being a naive seventeen-year-old without the confidence to challenge my treatment. Granted, I stood my ground in the room, defended myself, but I should have taken it further – how many other Black candidates didn't get through because of that woman's prejudices?

I know I was coming from a less powerful position, but so was Rosa Parks as she refused to give up her seat to a white man. Whichever standpoint I look at it from, I allowed racism to continue that day *by doing nothing*. And the worrying thing is, so many experiences like mine go unreported, because Black people don't want to rock the boat; it's easier to say and do nothing. I am a quite different person now, but that's not the point – this is one of the demons I have to face. I only wish I could turn the clock back.

But I was a woman who had had the stuffing knocked out of her. I could not change my life, *that was it for me*, I had to accept that all that awaited me was mediocrity.

THE FIRST TIME I WAS CALLED A 'NIGGER'

CHAPTER
XVIII

Racism was all around me, but as I was growing up the hatred that came with it did not directly affect me. When our family lived in Spring Hill, we became friends with our Jewish neighbours who never bothered us. Moving to Tottenham on to a street predominantly occupied by West Indians gave us an added safety net; we had each other. But we knew there were no-go areas, like Bethnal Green, Mile End and Stepney, with their strong National Front presence.

Thankfully, I had never been attacked or openly abused by someone racist. Of course, I had heard stories from friends who had been, but we were careful not to venture too far away from the area we knew. 'Let dem come down 'ere and see wat will happen to dem if dem bad,' Dad would say.

But in 1991, when I was in my twenty-seventh year, I experienced head-on the full force of racism. It was accepted in the Campbell family that there was an ongoing rivalry between my brothers and me when it came to football. I am and have always been a Tottenham Hotspur (Spurs) supporter whilst my brothers supported our arch-enemy, Arsenal. It was no easy task to support a team that had not won a trophy in years, particularly when dealing with smug, gloating brothers who took great pleasure in that fact. But the year 1991 was going to be different, with the two teams finally coming face to face in the FA Cup semi-final.

By now I was working as a housing benefit officer for Islington Council. I had a handful of good friends, both Black and white, amongst them my close and dear Italian friend, Emma. We had met at my previous job at the Department of Health and Social Security, and our friendship had blossomed over the years. Italians were similar to West Indians in how they brought up their children – strict but fair – and we would often share stories about our upbringing. I loved the Italian language – it was filled with life, every word and expression explosive. We would spend evenings in Emma's top-floor flat in Crouch End listening to Italian opera on vinyl records, and Emma would translate them for me. Although it was nice to know what the words meant, it sounded so much better in Italian.

Emma, like me, was a Spurs supporter and we suffered along with the other fans for years as Arsenal fans took great pleasure in rubbing our noses in the fact that we had not won a major trophy for over ten years. But when Spurs got to the semi-finals and it was announced the game was being held at Wembley, we were both determined to get tickets. So, Emma and I, with two of our white friends, Mark and Sam, took the day off work and got up in the early hours to queue up at White Hart Lane in Tottenham. The hours of waiting were worth it, as the four of us managed to get tickets. Afterwards we were so ecstatic that we spent the rest of the day eating, drinking and bowling. We bought our scarves and T-shirts – mine had 'Every Gunner's a Runner' plastered across it (Gunner is a nickname for Arsenal). My brothers were gutted. 'You should have got ya lazy backsides up like I did,' I told them smugly, not hiding my satisfaction in any way.

The final was to be held on Sunday 14 April, 1991. The day before the final, I made my way to Emma's flat to make arrangements. We had a great evening, and I left Emma's around nine o'clock. I was driving by then and had a red Ford Fiesta, which I took immense pride in. As I drove back to Tottenham, I came across a group of bikers. It looked like they were attending a bikers' rally or something because there were so many of them as they passed me. One of them came so close to my car that I shouted, 'Back off, you idiot!' The biker looked over at me and kicked my car door and then yelled, 'Shut up, you fucking nigger,' before laughing and speeding off.

When I heard the word, my heart skipped a beat. I was shocked but also petrified; he'd said it with such venom. I drove home in a daze, and I could not understand it, but I felt embarrassed by what had happened. I started to second-guess myself, wondering whether it was my fault for calling him an idiot. When I got home, I thought of calling my parents, but decided against it. *I didn't tell anyone.* It was such a lonely place – that heinous word struck at my dignity. Why didn't I say something, *do something*? Racism isolates you, even when you know other people experience it too.

I didn't get much sleep as I replayed what had happened, and when I met my friends the following day, I kept it to myself. Emma knew something was wrong, but racism is like a bad smell – no one wants to mention it because it's such an uncomfortable subject. Besides, I had been looking forward to this day and was not about to let some racist ruin it for me. The atmosphere at Wembley was electric, and thankfully it rubbed off on me. Arsenal were confident as the favourites because they were top of the Football League and, as usual, Spurs were lagging behind. The Arsenal fans were vocal in their belief that we didn't stand a chance, and as we considered how the two teams had performed that season, I could not help feeling a little nervous. When we got inside the stadium, we could not believe how close we were to the field – they were brilliant tickets.

When the two teams came out, the stadium erupted. But what happened next shocked us all, because within minutes Spurs midfielder Paul 'Gazza' Gascoigne scored, hitting the ball right into the back of the net from a free kick. The euphoria of that moment pushed any negative feelings about the incident the previous day to the back of my mind. Emma and I hugged and kissed, it was a wonderful feeling. When Spurs striker Gary Lineker scored to make it 2–0, we could not believe it. Arsenal managed to pull a goal back just before half-time to make it 2–1, but in the second half, Spurs sealed the win when Lineker scored his second goal, taking the final score to 3–1. We had beaten our arch-enemies and I could not wait to get back to my parents', where I knew my brothers were watching the match with Dad.

The Spurs fans made the most of their moment of glory, taking full advantage of the devastated Arsenal fans as they sang in chorus across Wembley:

You're not sing-ing,
You're not sing-ing,
You're not singing any more!
You're not singing a-ny-more!

We left the stadium triumphant and headed to Wood Green, where we had a couple of drinks in a local pub, at which point Sam and Mark decided they wanted a kebab. Emma and I decided against it but went along with them to the kebab shop. We made our way to the Tube station and were just approaching the shopping centre when a car and a motorbike suddenly screeched to a stop in front of us. A young Black man jumped out of the car and he and the young white guy who'd been riding the bike started fighting. It was happening right in front of us; they kicked and punched each other, and we watched in horror as the Black man got his opponent on to the floor and was getting the better of him. I shouted at them both to stop, but they were consumed with a blind rage. Emma was terrified, and Sam and Mark, along with everyone else, just looked on, dumbfounded.

At that moment another biker appeared. He called someone's name and pulled the Black guy off the white guy. The second biker was tall and well built. He knocked the Black guy to the ground, and I prayed it would be over. But the Black guy got up, strode to the boot of his car, flung it open, and pulled out his jack. He and the well-built biker rushed at each other again, and after a struggle, the white biker managed to prise the jack from his grip. He punched the Black guy, knocking him face-down to the ground. White biker jumped on him and began striking him on the back of the head with the jack, with each blow snarling, 'I'll teach you to come over 'ere, take our jobs, take our women!'

I screamed at him to stop. He wouldn't, so I did the only thing I could, I ran over to the large biker and screeched at him. At that moment he stopped, stood up and looked me straight in the eye, and I could not believe my eyes – *he was the same person who had called me 'nigger' the day before*. But this time, I was not scared or embarrassed, I was just mad. 'Don't just stand there,' I shouted out to everyone. 'Do something, call the police!' It was at that point the other biker grabbed his friend and shouted, 'Come on, let's go.' The two men jumped on their bikes and sped off. The Black guy was moaning, barely conscious, bleeding profusely from the back of his head. I wrapped my Tottenham scarf around his head and waited with him until the ambulance arrived. I wanted to go with him in the ambulance, but Emma begged me to stay out of it. I knew he was in good hands, and I had to admit I had witnessed him taking the jack out of his car, which was wrong. But the hatred between the man and the bikers had been amplified by racism. I didn't want to be a part of that, and even if the case were to go to court and I was required to give evidence, the Black guy's actions would not have helped him, so I walked away.

As the four of us made our way home, there was silence. I think Emma was shocked I would put myself at risk like that for someone I didn't know, but she had no idea about the incident the day before, and I had no intention of telling her. I should have asked them what they thought about the barrage of racist abuse from the bikers, but the Black man was equally to blame for the violence, so I did not want to look as if I was justifying his actions in any way. Luckily, Emma and I were too close for anything to put a wedge between us, and I know that she was only concerned for my safety. We are as close today as we ever were.

'The bwoy is stupid, why him 'ave to tek out a weapon? He should 'ave kick dat racist white bwoy's backside and a go 'bout im business,' Dad said in a matter-of-fact way, as I told my parents what had happened. Of course, I was extremely diplomatic, omitting the part about how I got into the thick of it, which would have only gotten Dad hopping mad and given Mum a nervous breakdown. I told them only what they needed to know. As for my brothers, they were nowhere to be found. Hiding in shame after their team had been beaten into oblivion by Spurs.

That night I lay awake thinking about a weekend that had been filled with such highs and lows. *Was it the same guy?* That would be too much of a coincidence. Was I psychologically traumatised by what had happened to me the day before; did I see what I wanted to see? Whether it was the same guy or not, was there any difference between one racist and another?

Those two incidents did something to me. It was as if I'd been re-booted, kicked back into touch with reality. I was mad, *really mad*, that, despite having been born here, having lived my life as best I could, I still had to put up with this shit! I gained a new consciousness – I no longer wanted to sit on the sidelines; I wanted to confront these issues head on.

I was a member of the union at Islington Council at the time and joined the Black Workers Group. It was not that militant, but it did highlight what was happening to Black employees within the Council, and I became a vocal member, attending all the meetings and providing information on matters of importance. Within a few months I had become a regular face at the meetings and was eventually voted in as Secretary.

The role came with much responsibility. As well as chairing meetings, I was required to act as an advocate for Black staff facing disciplinaries, which involved going through the evidence against them together and acting for them at hearings. At first, I was extremely nervous — what if I let them down and they lost their jobs? Luckily, no case ever got that serious. My presentation skills were good, and it was a fantastic feeling to finally be able to make a difference. I had always dreamed of being a lawyer, and acting officially for Council employees in the Black Workers Group was the next best thing. I gained confidence, which reflected on my progress at work as I attended benefit appeal hearings on behalf of the Council. I would prepare and present cases to Councillors, and although officers were rarely successful, I won all my cases. I had no idea how far this newfound confidence and self-awareness was going to take me.

THE
PLUS
PRO—
GRAMME

CHAPTER XIX

Joyce and I were born only one year and three months apart. As the older sister, she never lets me forget it. Growing up, we did everything together. 'Dem look just alike,' people would regularly say. Once, Joyce threw a party, and the photographer she had booked spoke to me for at least five minutes before he realised that I was not my sister. 'Are you twins?' we were often asked, and we would shake our heads and say no.

When we were both still in primary school, we would go to Girl Guides on a Monday evening. I must have been nine or ten. The Guides was just a short walk away in Stamford Hill, so Mum would let Joyce and I go together by ourselves. One night on the way to the Guides, we were crossing at the main road. We approached the busy junction, and, for a split second, I let go of Joyce's hand. That's when both of us were hit by a car. Joyce was thrown across the road towards oncoming traffic. I was lying on the road with people all around me. I screamed for my sister, and I don't know where he came from, but, all of a sudden, a police officer grabbed Joyce and put her on the pavement. There was chaos, people were shouting and all I wanted to do was get to my sister. Within minutes an ambulance arrived, and we were bundled away to the hospital.

Mum said the sense of dread she felt when the police arrived at her door and told her and Dad what had happened was 'crippling'. When my parents, Fitz and Glen arrived at the hospital and saw us both laid up in a cubicle dressed in white

hospital gowns, they started to cry, 'Lard Jesus, Lard Jesus . . . '
Thank God, after being x-rayed we were cleared to go home,
suffering from shock, cuts and bruises.

Dad being Dad drove us all to the junction where it happened
and made us explain to him what we had done, before going
through in detail about what we needed to do when crossing
such a busy junction. Needless to say, we were never allowed to
go to Girl Guides again. That officer saved Joyce from serious
injury or, God forbid, even worse.

The police had looked after us until the ambulance arrived and
then had the job of going to my parents to tell them what had
happened. That good impression was embedded in my mind
and I carry it with me wherever I go. It was to be followed by
more negative ones, though, as I'd watch my twelve-year-old
brother being searched on his way home from school, whilst
still in his school uniform, and as police vans patrolling the area
became a regular feature. By the time I'd reached this new sense
of awareness, I wanted to find out more about the organisation
that had impacted my community. The Black community cannot escape the fact that the police represent law and order in
Britain, and they are all we have, whether we trust them or not.

In 1987, the Metropolitan Police were about to get a shake-up,
the likes of which they had never seen. Police accountability was
to be placed in the foreground, which was to give me some hope
that at last things were about to change. Throughout my journey,
one thing has remained constant – change cannot occur unless
those in positions of responsibility are prepared to adapt, to be
more innovative in their thinking.

Sir Peter Imbert became the Commissioner of the Metropolitan Police on 1 January, 1987, after holding various senior roles
within the force. In 1979, he was Chief Constable of Thames
Valley Police, the youngest Chief Constable in the country. During
his time at Thames Valley, Imbert allowed the BBC to make

Police, a 1982 fly-on-the-wall documentary series about the police at work. The opposite of a public relations exercise, it exposed the flaws in Thames Valley policing when an episode of the programme showed three detectives interrogating and dismissing a rape victim. In response, and to effect change within the force, Imbert instigated improvements to the handling of rape cases at Thames Valley, which were adopted throughout the country. This established a crucial aspect of Imbert's management skills: the ability to recognise the need for change, and to act upon it to ensure the victim's needs were considered within that difficult legal process.

Imbert took on the role as Commissioner with the same ideals in respect of transparency. He wanted the police to be more open and accessible to the public, stating at a police conference in 1989 that, 'Openness must be central to the policing of a democratic and pluralist society.'[169] With that in mind he commissioned specialists to undertake an audit of internal and external attitudes towards the Metropolitan Police (the Met).[170] The final report titled 'A Force for Change' drew on over 250 formal interviews and concluded that the Met needed to improve its communication techniques, both internally and with the world outside.[171] To be effective there needed to be a culture change within the Met.

The report resulted in the development of the PLUS programme, which included the development of the 'Statement of Common Purpose and Values'. PLUS focused on improving leadership and the quality of service, attempting to change the police culture with a series of seminars to all 44,000 staff members at a cost of £5.5 million. Imbert also changed the name from Metropolitan Police Force to Metropolitan Police Service. PLUS encouraged 'openness', and the public were to be seen and treated as consumers and as the customer. Through the new programme there was a realisation from the police that it needed to reconsider its relationship with the public.[172]

On Imbert's death in November 2017, writer for the *Independent*, Nick Hobbs said: 'No other senior officer has ever implemented such a far-reaching programme of self-assessment.'[173] His style of leadership was popular and pragmatic, doing much to restore his force's pride in itself and reputation with the public. At the same time, he had moved the organisation forward, especially in the fields of race and diversity, and quality management. The PLUS programme was a landmark in engineering cultural change. But, due to internal opposition and serious illness Imbert retired at the end of 1992, which would mean an end to the PLUS programme ideals.

There is no telling what bridges might have been built between the Black community and the police had Imbert's PLUS initiative not been cut short. There is no doubt it would have taken time, but Imbert's forward thinking and willingness to retrain officers within the police service in such vast numbers showed a commitment to working towards breaking down barriers. Sadly, we will never know how far his revolutionary PLUS programme could have taken us.

In 1993 Imbert was succeeded by Paul Condon. At the heart of PLUS's aims lay a simple principle: 'that both internally, and in their dealings with the public, the police had to be more democratic, more ready to listen to criticism, less hierarchical and authoritarian.'[174] Under the programme, senior officers were no longer judges in their cause – their subordinates and customers were equally important and had the right to question their judgement. One of Condon's early acts was to see an end to the PLUS programme, which was downgraded and then abolished. The distance between ranks was reasserted, and the negative elements of canteen culture tightened their grip.[175]

Under Condon, the Met became a less open institution. This renewed detachment from the public as a whole could not have come at a worse time.

STEPHEN

CHAPTER
XX

On 22 April, 1993, eighteen-year-old aspiring architect Stephen Lawrence was killed by a gang of white men in an unprovoked racist attack. He had been waiting for a bus in Eltham, South-east London, with a friend when the gang attacked them. Stephen's friend Duwayne Brooks escaped unhurt, but Stephen died from his injuries. The police initially investigated Neil and Jamie Acourt, Gary Dobson, David Norris and Luke Knight, who they believed were responsible for the attack. Neil Acourt and Luke Knight were identified by Duwayne Brooks as being a part of the gang that attacked them, and the pair were charged with murder. On 29 July, 1993, the Crown Prosecution Service dropped the prosecution, stating that the identification evidence from Brooks was unreliable. In September 1994, Stephen's parents launched a private prosecution against Gary Dobson, Luke Knight, and Neil Acourt, but were unsuccessful when the case went to the Old Bailey in 1996, with charges dropped for lack of evidence.

But in the midst of this, the Metropolitan Police Commissioner Paul Condon ignited a further row — which was only to reinforce negative stereotypes of Black people — when in 1995 he wrote to MPs and forty community groups, including the Commission for Racial Equality, calling on leaders of ethnic minority communities to recognise that the majority of muggings in London were carried out by young Black males.[176] At the time, Labour MP Bernie Grant accused Condon of pandering to racism, whilst criminologists treated such statements with caution. But was there something more sinister behind Condon's actions? It was just a few months before the private prosecution for the murder of Stephen Lawrence was due to take place. The police were under immense pressure, faced with serious criticisms of their handling of the case. Was this a strategic move on his part, to distract attention from the responsibility of the police and place it squarely at the door of the Black community?

In July 1998, after years of fighting for justice for their son, the Lawrence family called for the resignation of Paul Condon, who in October of that year stated, 'I deeply regret we have not brought Stephen's racist murderers to justice and I would like to personally apologise today to Mr and Mrs Lawrence for our failure.'[177]

Stephen Lawrence was just four years younger than my brother Glen, and both his parents were Jamaican like my parents, and had made a life for themselves in Britain. Every West Indian family was affected by the death of Stephen. Because everyone knew it could just as easily have been one of them. To us as a community, it was hard enough to lose a child, but we also had to live with what could only be described as the indifference of the police to the death of a Black teenager. It was as though none of them cared that the murderers were being allowed to go free. The police were all we had, they were supposed to represent law and order. But what Stephen's case showed was that for us there was no justice for us. The murder investigation could not have been more different to PC Keith Blakelock's. Both he and Stephen Lawrence were human beings who had a right to justice, but in 1985 the police were prepared to move heaven and earth to find Blakelock's killers. It was not believed that the rift between the police and the Black community could get any wider, but the failings on the part of the police when it came to Stephen Lawrence's murder resulted in an even bigger rift.

In 1998, a public inquiry headed by Sir William MacPherson examined the original Metropolitan Police Service investigation,

and in 1999, the MacPherson Report was published, citing a cata-
logue of errors in how the investigation had been conducted and
concluding that the force had been 'marred by a combination of
professional incompetence, institutional racism and a failure
of leadership'.[178] A total of 70 recommendations designed to show
'zero tolerance' for racism in society were made. They included
measures not just to transform the attitude of the police towards
race relations and improve accountability but also to get the Civil
Service, NHS, judiciary, and other public bodies to respond and
change.

More than twenty years on from the MacPherson recommendations, National Statistics for 2020 reveal that within the Civil
Service workforce, 320,580 employees are white compared to
just 12,800 Black employees.[179] Within the NHS, in very senior
management roles for non-medical staff, statistics reveal that
92.6 per cent are white, and 1.3 per cent Black, accounting for
just 28 roles. In relation to consultants within the NHS, 59.9 per
cent are white, and 2.9 per cent are Black, making up just 1,437
compared to 29,940 white consultants.[180] Within the legal profession, 92.6 per cent of court judges are white and just 1.1 per
cent Black.[181] Recommendations have no real power unless those
responsible for implementing them are prepared to change. The
above figures illustrate the ongoing reluctance to change.

It would take nineteen years for Gary Dobson and David Norris
to be convicted of Stephen's murder in January 2012, following
Stephen's DNA being found on their clothes. What would have
happened in the Stephen Lawrence case if the PLUS programme
had been in place? Would things have been different? Twenty
-five years on from Stephen's death, Chief Constable Jon
Boutcher, the National Police Chiefs' Council lead on race and
religion, stated that police forces have been too slow to improve
their record on race. Boutcher told the *Guardian*, 'There have
been the words, but not the actions. We need to make sure we
have words and actions.' [182]

MY LEGAL JOURNEY BEGINS

CHAPTER
XXI

In 1998, I was in my early thirties, but there was an underlying discontent that I couldn't shake. My involvement in the Black Workers Group and watching everything unfold in the Lawrence case had continued to kindle my sense of self. I had become comfortable with *being safe*. It was easier to believe that I didn't deserve more; this was my lot. But you can lie to everyone, never to yourself, and each day brought fresh doubts about the life I had *settled for*. I had left Islington Council in 1997 and was now working as agency staff in the Hackney benefits team. At the beginning of the year, I felt a determination to change my life, find something that would fulfil me. I read up on the different courses that might work for me; my love for English swayed me towards an English Literature degree. But what would I do with a degree like that once I qualified? Would I go into teaching? I decided that entering a classroom filled with teenagers at that time of life was not for me. Then there was the law, *my dream*. But, was I good enough to get in? The University of North London, now a part of London Metropolitan University, was enrolling for September of that year, so I applied and took the entrance test on a rainy Tuesday afternoon. I read a legal case and then answered questions on it, and this time, unlike the police exam, I passed. In September 1998, I began a full-time law degree.

As by now I had a mortgage and ongoing bills, I needed to continue working. The timetable at University of North London required attendance at lectures and workshops in the mornings, and some afternoons. A great manager allowed me to effectively arrange my working hours around university, as long as I was able to continue working for at least twenty-five hours a week. I agreed, and for the next three years my white Cavalier SRi, (which replaced my red Ford Fiesta) and I would drive between work and university, with every weekend spent in the university library. Those three years went by so quickly, and at times I questioned my decision to study full time whilst holding down a job. But a part-time evening course would have taken six years and I had wasted enough time.

Emma and those friends closest to me remained loyal, even though I wasn't able to see them very often. My life became consumed by books and there was no such thing as a social life. Being a mature student was an experience; the young people within my year were free-spirited. The law degree was important to them, but a social life was equally important. They would be making arrangements to hit a club, or go drinking, and were always skint. I made quite a few friends and as an older student I was often asked to provide advice on one thing or another.

My lecturers were amazing. Some of them were concerned that I had taken on too much, but they always had time to answer any questions I had about a particular topic. It was crucial that I secured a First or an Upper Second Class degree if I was going to have a chance of finding a job within the legal profession. I stayed up all night more than once to complete urgent assignments because the following week would be filled with hitting required hours at work. One advantage of being so experienced was that it enabled me to obtain work as the housing benefit court officer in my final year, which counted towards one of my modules, something I took full advantage of. My parents worried about me a lot because they hardly saw me, and I had little time for my sisters and brothers. I fell out of favour quite a lot during those three years.

But it was all worth it when in 2001 I left North London University with an Upper Second Class Honours LLB. I continued to work for Hackney Council as a housing benefit officer, as I needed to finance the Legal Practice Course, a mandatory professional course that cost in excess of £8,000. I could not wait to get out of the benefits department, and I asked a friend who knew someone in the legal department to put me in touch, in the hope of getting some legal experience as a legal admin officer. A meeting was set up and I met a white man who worked as a lawyer within the department. He listened patiently as I told him about my background and my experience, and how I had studied full-time whilst holding down a job. He seemed impressed, but at the end of it he said, 'I don't know why people with perfectly good jobs want a job in law.'

His words hit me hard. Nothing I'd said about my difficult journey had made any difference. With one sentence he dismissed me, taking me back to that classroom where my teacher told me I was not A level material. *Settle for what you've got*. That's effectively what he meant. But I had no intention of *settling*, and I walked out of that room knowing that if I wanted to get a job in legal, I would have to go elsewhere. I was now very different to that fifteen-year-old girl, or that seventeen-year-old who had been humiliated in the Army recruitment office. I was no longer that young woman of twenty-one who'd been belittled by being asked why I hadn't applied to join a West Indian airline.

It took me just under a year to save up the money for the Legal Practice Course at the College of Law in Store Street, just off Tottenham Court Road. At the age of thirty-seven, I left Hackney Council and became a full-time student. I was a little apprehensive, walking away from paid employment, but with careful financial planning I was able to pay my mortgage and bills. The students at the College of Law were mainly young white males. I didn't make any real friends there; my objective was to get through the course and move on to the next stage of my journey. The college offered a career service, and after a few months I booked an appointment. The career adviser was quite blunt, and said, 'There are jobs . . . voluntary organisations could be useful and there are always offices on the high street.' She didn't ask me what area of law I was interested in – she obviously thought I should take what I could get. I wasn't surprised by her response because it was all too familiar. I had come this far, however, and was not about to stop now. So, I thanked her and left.

It took nine months to complete my Legal Practice Course, and in 2002 I passed at the age of thirty-eight.

Then came the biggest hurdle: I had to find a legal firm to take me on as a trainee solicitor. A number of doubters came out of the woodwork, only too keen to tell me I would never make it, because I was too old, I was Black, and I was a woman. I took those words and flipped them, replacing 'too old' with 'experienced', 'Black' with 'powerful, resilient and tenacious', and 'woman' with . . . well, the strength of character of women past and present, my mother being at the top of the list. Besides, I thought, you might get a million 'no's, but all you needed was one 'yes'.

I searched through the *Yellow Pages* and carefully took down the address of every solicitor's office in the London area. I proceeded to send my CV with a cover letter and stamped addressed envelope to every one. I received just twenty replies, all saying thanks, but no thanks. By now, I had returned to work as a housing benefit officer. That was the hardest time, because it came with so many disappointments. Each rejection letter brought a new low. But I brushed myself down and started again, even after the time I sat up all night completing an application form to meet the deadline, only to be told that the wrong postage had been attached. I had paid 72 pence and it should have been 82 pence. I begged them to accept my application: 'I'll pay the extra,' I told them. But they refused, saying it would not be fair on the other candidates. I cried for a week as I considered all the hard work I had put in, only to lose out for the sake of 10 pence.

I read law magazines, and religiously checked newspapers for vacant legal positions. One day I was looking through the legal section of the *Guardian* newspaper and came across a feature about a young woman who had secured a training contract in Her Majesty's Court Service, working as a legal adviser within the Magistrates' Court. The difference with these contracts was that they were aimed at people who had previous work experience and could think on their feet, because they'd be required to advise magistrates on the law and run the courts. A contract like that was perfect for me, and from that moment I searched for every vacancy I could find. The competition in London was fierce and opportunities were scarce, so I also looked outside London. When I saw a job in Kent, I applied and was shortlisted for interview. I took the train to West Malling, a quaint market town. I saw horses and sheep; it was vastly different to the Tottenham I grew up in.

The interview was conducted by two Chief Justice clerks, both white males. They were pleasant and I gave my presentation on anti-social behaviour, and then answered some questions on bail applications and other legal issues. Then came the final question, 'Why should we give you this job?' I had the bog-standard answer in my head; the usual, 'I'd be an asset' and 'I'm willing to work hard'. But when it came to it, I realised I needed to tell them the things that were different about me, the things that made me strong, so I simply said, 'Because I am unique, and I do not believe that you will have any other candidate like me. Life's about taking on new challenges and experiencing new things.' There was no arrogance behind the words, just a straightforward truth.

I got the job in April 2004. I had to drive from Tottenham through Maidstone, Sevenoaks, and Sittingbourne. I was one of only two Black legal advisers, running the courts and advising lay magistrates on the law. I had spent so much time searching for that elusive training contract that I never considered what a culture shock it would be to work outside London, a place where diversity was part and parcel of my life. It took me a while to acclimatise to an environment in which I was in the minority. For weeks I wasn't sure how to act, felt awkward away from what I had grown used to, but the only way I would survive was to be true to who I was. I had to *be me*. And, in taking that step, things became easier. It was also good for my colleagues to find out more about me and my family, and I too learned from them, and that experience taught me that we should not be afraid to spread our wings.

It was also important to be bold, not to be afraid to point out little things that a predominantly white organisation would not consider in respect of their Black staff. One of my duties required me to run the video link court, which dealt with people on remand in prison as they awaited trial. The Crown Prosecution Service and their legal representative would attend court and the defendants would attend from prison over the link. My first video link court took place within a few months of me starting. Although I had received full training, I had never actually been on camera myself. When the day arrived, I was quite nervous, but I just got on with it.

It was only when I logged into the camera that I noticed I looked extremely dark. The lighting had not factored in the need to compensate for a dark-skinned person. It was awful, and the problem was made worse by the fact that I was wearing a white shirt. All that could be seen on camera was my white shirt and white teeth. I felt sick and could literally hear the prison guards and the defendants laughing on the other side of the link. *I wanted to dig a hole and jump into it*. Not because I was ashamed of being Black, but because there was nothing, I could do to remedy that distorted image. I sat through four cases that afternoon and they seemed to last forever.

Pauline's graduation day on admittance to the roll of solicitors in 2004

Aftwerwards, I went straight to my manager and made it clear that I would not appear on another video link until the lighting had been adjusted. She was extremely apologetic and ensured the problem was sorted out within a week. What that experience showed me was that, although any offence was unintentional, in this context the white community lived in ignorance of the diversity around them. When the video link was originally set up, no consideration was given to a dark-skinned Black person using it. Work practices were not open to inclusion, which they should have been, whether there were Black employees or not. We all learned a lot from that experience, but the humiliation of that day is something that has stayed with me.

Those eighteen months were long and arduous, having to cover court, sometimes not finishing until after five, and then having to write up the cases before making the long hour-and-a-half journey back to Tottenham. I could not ignore the detrimental effect my working so far away from home had on my parents; Mum, in particular, would call me, out of her mind with worry, when she heard about a pile-up on a motorway. Winter months were extremely difficult for her, as she knew I was driving home late in the evening on either the M2, M20 or M25 after a long day in court. I would also be required to arrive early, because it was necessary to go through the court list with the magistrates as the legal adviser.

I worked in the criminal, civil, family and youth courts. It was the best training contract I could have hoped for because it taught me all I needed to know about the court service and how it worked. Like with any job, there were good and bad days, but thankfully the good days outweighed the bad.

I qualified at the age of forty-one in 2005 and took the next step into the legal world.

A
NEW
LIFE

CHAPTER XXII

The day I qualified as a lawyer was the day, I left Kent. I entered the office to find my desk covered with cards and balloons, and colourful decorations. My colleagues laid on a wonderful spread for lunch, and my boss, the Chief Justice clerk, and his wife sang a Welsh song during the presentation. It was overwhelming, just how many friends I had made in those eighteen months. Some wanted me to move to Kent, which would have enabled me to continue working there. I thought about it. My flat in London would have fetched a good price and I could have found a nice property in Kent, where the quality of life was better, what with the green fields and gorgeous views.

Making that decision would have changed my life, taken me into a new social environment, but it would also have taken me away from my family and friends. As tempting as the thought was, I was a *London girl*, and that could never change. No matter how well-meaning my white colleagues were, they had no idea how important my culture was to me. Maybe if I were white, it would have been easier to pick up sticks and move to a new, less diverse area outside London. But as a Black woman, I wanted to be around the people and things I knew.

'You want me to move down here? Show me where there's a Black hairdresser's,' I probed. 'Can any of you cook like my mum?' I continued. Although we all laughed about it, I was serious. I was aware that Black people did move into predominantly white areas, and this was a choice they made. *But I couldn't be one of them.* Maybe I was frightened of stepping into a new life, but as I got into the car, so full of presents I had to squeeze in, there were no doubts. I was now unemployed, but I had saved enough money to last a few months. It was clear that, having only just qualified, I would not walk straight into a lawyer's job. It was October 2006, I was forty-one years old, and I needed to find my first job as a lawyer, with no legal experience other than my legal training. *Scary times!*

It would have been easy to slip back into a housing benefit role, there was always work, but I was determined to find a job elsewhere and not fall back into the same old comfortable routine. Therefore, I signed up with some legal agencies as a newly qualified lawyer. For someone coming out of training, my CV was pretty impressive, with evidence of work experience and of extensive training within the courts. But a legal job did not fall into my lap and, in order to survive, I took on short-term agency work as a corporate complaints officer at Southwark Council. It was a good job, but when the permanent position became available and they asked me to apply, I declined. This too was a safe bet, taking me away from what I truly wanted. I had been on the legal agency's books for a few months, but I was not about to give up. Once again, I was unemployed.

I was out of work for about six weeks when I received a call from the legal agency telling me that a job had come up that was, in their words, made for me. And when they sent through the details, I could not believe it. The role was prosecuting lawyer for the London Borough of Hounslow, working on housing benefit prosecutions. If ever a job was made for anyone, this one was indeed made for me. I was asked in for an interview, where I met the principal lawyer within the litigation team, and once she saw how experienced I was, I got the job. The irony is not lost on me that, although once qualified I did everything I could to move away from housing benefit, the first legal job as a lawyer that I obtained was because of my housing benefit experience.

The only downside was that Hounslow was a long journey, at the other end of the Piccadilly line, and travelling back and forth on a busy tube could be pretty heavy going, but, at forty-two, this was my chance to begin my life as a lawyer. So I grabbed it.

As a trainee solicitor, you are lowest in the pecking order, and when you complete your training that's when you get the chance to build on your experience. But I had no idea how different my life would be as a lawyer. When I first met the investigation officers that I would work with and they found out about my background, heard my cockney accent and learned that I was an older Black woman who had worked her way through the Council as a benefits officer, there was a level of respect that I had not had before. To them, I had *been there, done that and wore the T-shirt*. It was not about me being the lawyer and them being the officers, it was about *us*, working together. They would speak to me about anything and everything. They trusted me because they knew I understood where they were coming from, which made my job ten times easier. It didn't matter that most of the staff were white; they saw me as *one of them*. As well as housing benefit, I was also required to deal with education and general criminal cases as and when required.

I loved attending Ealing and Brentford Magistrates' Courts, where I would get to my feet and represent my clients. This sometimes involved dealing with somewhat difficult defence lawyers who made it clear they had a dislike for local authorities. But I felt no nerves going from being the legal adviser of the court to the prosecutor. I had cut my teeth in court, so knew the system inside out. But, as with Kent, Hounslow was not known for having many Black lawyers in court, and, unfortunately, being mistaken for the list caller became a common occurrence. 'No, I'm not the list caller,' was something I would find myself saying so often that my annoyance turned to resignation.

I worked in Hounslow for six months. Although I enjoyed it, the pay was quite low for the work I was doing. When I asked my principal if there was the chance of a raise because of my experience and she offered an extra £1 an hour, I decided it would be best to look elsewhere.

I did not feel that I was being selfish or ungrateful for the opportunity I'd been given, but after everything I had been through, I was adamant that I should know my worth. I had researched the area of work I was doing and knew that the going rate was at least £7 more an hour. By settling for less I would have devalued myself, something I was determined never to do again.

I had always wanted to work for a bigger firm near the City, and with that in mind I contacted one of the more prestigious agencies. I spoke to a lady over the phone after sending in my CV, who told me, 'Maybe you should try another agency, I don't think you are quite what we are looking for.' I was angry and I wanted to tell her where she could stick my CV, but, as I'd reasoned after my failure to get into the police, how happy would I have been working for an agency that clearly had such a limited scope?

Two weeks after that rejection, I received a call from none other than Hackney Council, who were looking for a lawyer. I did not think twice about going for it; after all, it was close to home, the area was culturally diverse and I would get to see my friends who still worked there. This time there was no dismissal, I did not even have to go into the office, because the interview was conducted over the phone. I got the job. And at the age of forty-three, I walked through the doors of Hackney Council offices as a lawyer.

I was a lawyer with Hackney for twelve years. I was feisty and passionate about my job – I would be at my desk at six every morning and still be there twelve hours later. I had an excellent multicultural team and some wonderful clients. Under my leadership we became an award-winning team and were shortlisted for prestigious awards. As an accredited trainer, I also had the opportunity to train lawyers and investigating officers from across the country. On one occasion I made my way to Oxford, arriving early in order to prepare. I met the organiser who took me to the room in which the training would take place. There was someone already there, a white man reading a paper. The lady turned to me and said, 'Oh that's good, at least the trainer's arrived.'

'No, I'm the trainer,' I told her. She turned beetroot red and apologised. Instead of anger, there was frustration that no matter how far we had come, *I had come*, this stubborn, embedded preconception of Black people's capabilities remained. That day, I took great pleasure in dispelling any doubts *anyone* had about my ability.

As a Black lawyer, you get used to walking into a room and seeing the shock on people's faces when they meet you for the first time. 'Oh, so *you're* Miss Campbell!' they say, which tells me I am not who they were expecting. When entering court, I am required to go through security. On one occasion, I had to leave some perfume behind the security desk as I was prohibited from bringing it into court. After my hearing, I returned to collect it and got chatting with one of the guards. He asked if I had had a good day, I told him yes, and then he asked what department I worked for. It didn't offend me in any way, because we would regularly ask each other what we did when we were in court. I said to him, 'Why don't you guess.' He thought for a moment and then reeled off a number of commendable professions, 'Social worker, probation officer, housing officer. . . ' The list went on and on, but at no point did he say *lawyer*. When he had exhausted himself and I eventually revealed my profession, he said, 'No, really?' From that moment on, when someone, whatever the setting, asks me what I do for a living I always ask them to guess, and in all this time no one has ever got it right. The most enlightening part of this is that I'm not just talking about white people but Asians as well as Black people, which gives some indication of how we value not only ourselves, but each other.

In 2009, whilst attending the Notting Hill Carnival I bumped into an old flame. I had no idea at the time that he would become my future husband. Everton is a tall, strapping six-foot-two Sheffield lad, whose parents came to the UK from Jamaica in the 1960s. Everton moved to London in 1993 and worked in housing. He grew up in an area where Blacks were in the minority and spent a lot of his young life running from racist white youths. One day, he and his friends were being chased and he suddenly decided, 'I've had enough of running.' So he stopped and confronted the white youths. He knew that because he was outnumbered it was not going to end well, but he was determined to get a few punches in. As they approached, he prepared himself, but at that moment a group of police pulled up, and the youths scattered. 'Usually, the police were the last people you wanted to see, but that night, lass, I was glad when they turned that chuffing corner,' he said, but he also told me that from the moment he stopped running he felt empowered. We would talk for hours about our lives, and how similar our experiences were, despite our having grown up hundreds of miles away from each other. As a child he was encouraged to get a job within the Sheffield steel industry, but this was not for him. Coming to London was his chance to move away from the life he had known and finding a job in housing provided him with a more hopeful future.

We were married in 2018. My brothers Fitz and Glen walked me down the aisle. We argued all the way as they told me to slow down, but I just wanted to get to him. 'Lard Jesus, I wish yu daddy were here,' Mum cried. Anne was overcome with happiness as she took her place alongside the family, and Joyce, being the amazing events planner she is, organised the entire wedding, timing everything with precision. It was the most wonderful day. I missed my dad, but for me, he was there in spirit.

A NEW BEGINNING SPARKED BY A TRAGIC END

CHAPTER
XXIII

When I lost Dad, it was like being on a ship without a compass. His guidance and wisdom were invaluable to us as a family; his passing left a void. It also became clear that I had lost sight of what was important, *really important*. It had taken so long to become a solicitor that once I attained the position it became my main focus. I saw my family, but I put my career first. It was only after Dad died that I was able to reflect on my life and consider what a significant role racism had played in it, and also in the lives of my parents and a whole generation brought up on rice and peas and fish and chips.

Could we have done anything differently, fought harder to reach our goals? Did we, as a generation, lack the intellectual prowess to succeed? The answer to that question is a resounding *NO*. We were a generation that politicians and institutions utilised to their own ends, laying unemployment, lack of housing and high crime rates squarely at our door. As for intellectual prowess, that's the biggest myth of all; becoming a solicitor has shown me that the starting point has to be a belief in yourself. But lack of opportunity because of teachers' or employers' preconceived ideas – their inability to be adaptable and flexible in their thinking – has played a key role in limiting our choices, and any attempt to address the imbalance such as Race Relations legislation, the Rampton Report on Education, the Scarman or MacPherson Reports, has been met with resistance.

On 25 May, 2020, during the killer global coronavirus pandemic, something happened that would show the ultimate evil of racism in its purest and deadliest form – the knee of a police officer was pressed into the neck of George Floyd for *eight minutes and forty-six seconds* with such ferocity that it ended his life. George Floyd's murder, shared on video through social media before being televised, sent shock waves throughout the world. Perhaps the most disturbing aspect of this heinous crime is that it illustrates how lonely the experience of racism is. It did not matter that millions of people watched in sheer horror as George Floyd's life ebbed away, because throughout those awful moments *he was alone*.

As everyone is when they're subjected to racism – standing in a queue, on the bus or train, walking home, working at your desk, or, in my case, being called 'a nigger' as you sit in your car – when it happens *it only happens to you*. And when you speak of it, your voice is only heard in a whisper. But after George Floyd was murdered, suddenly, *everyone* was listening.

In the year of my birth, I was welcomed into the world with the slogan 'If you want a nigger for a neighbour vote Labour.'[183] At the age of three I was described as 'a wide-grinning piccaninny' by our nemesis Enoch Powell, who warned it would be dangerous to integrate us into British society and went on to see us children as a threat in his infamous speech of 1968, which secured his place in history.[184] I was a teenager as I watched the streets of Brixton light up in 1981. Four years later, I was to find police on every corner after the riots on Broadwater Farm Estate in Tottenham that ended the life of PC Keith Blakelock. And I watched as the police unleashed their own retribution on the Black community in which I lived.

'Racism' is like a four-letter word that we dare not speak aloud, because, once we do, we're in the spotlight. We can't be sure of the response we're going to get, or whether that response will adequately address the complaint. It's often a case of being accused of having a chip on your shoulder, or of being disregarded or ignored. Or of being told on prime-time TV,

'It's getting boring now.'[185] A lot of the time, encountering racism, and considering how to challenge it, comes with a sense weariness. *What's the point*, we think, *I'm not going to be heard*. Succumbing to these feeling, though, could make matters worse, and result in the racism not actually being addressed. It gives the perpetrators ammunition to make life more difficult for the target. Some of us play ball by deracialising ourselves, making ourselves more acceptable within the organisation. It's safer not to raise a concern that might label your manager a racist, because if you did, they would only get defensive, and in turn label you a troublemaker, invariably leading to your own work performance being questioned. But there are those of us who are prepared to take desperate measures to escape the inequality of being Black.

In the modern-day Caribbean, the belief that lighter skin will open doors is more prevalent than ever as bleaching among dark-skinned Jamaicans is being taken to extreme levels.[186] Young women are mixing dangerous cocktails of products, some of which are illegal in the UK, including Bio Claire and Caro White creams; Neoprosone and Haloderm, made in Switzerland, creams like Idole, made in Spain. Powerful gels containing two types of steroids – betamethasone, and neomycin sulphate – and Volume 40 lotions, such as Clarins White, or Raid Glow meant for hair but used because of its strengthening qualities that speed up the skin lightening process in addition to hydrogen peroxide. The harmful concoction is pasted over the entire body, and the skin is then wrapped in plastic, as sweat accelerates the lightening process, and covered with six to ten layers of clothing, including thick gloves, despite the baking heat. This ritual can take place up to three times a day.

In the quest to become a 'bare brownie', dark-skinned Jamaicans risk what they describe as 'bursting', where the skin stretches and tears, leaving the veins more exposed, which some try to conceal with tattoos. The treatment can also lead to dark patches and severe scarring. For most it does work, but as the applications continue, the skin becomes a greying pink.

Research and Market, the world's largest market research store, has revealed that the global skin-lightening market is projected to reach 12.3 billion dollars by the year 2027.[187] Japan represents the largest market worldwide, with the World Health Organization confirming that Nigeria tops the list of the percentage of women in the African countries using skin-lightening products, amounting to 77 per cent, with high numbers also reported in the Caribbean.

Those who lighten their skin are victims of racism. They have no idea that this belief that white skin is superior has been entrenched going back centuries, a myth created in which Black people have been demoralised and degraded, described as intellectually inferior in order to justify the act of slavery. Racism isn't about the colour of your skin, it's about the right to privilege and opportunity. A light-skinned enslaved person living in their master's house is still an enslaved person, can still be raped, have their children taken away and sold, and be prohibited from learning to read. We have enough to contend with in respect of racism – why are we so eager to initiate a colour divide amongst ourselves?

Growing up I used to think Black people must have done something really bad for such inequality to exist. At the time, it was easy to fall into the trap of believing the police were the catalyst for the injustice that had befallen our community, but as I grew into a sense of consciousness on this enlightening journey, sparked by the loss of my dad, it became clear the police were just one part of a well-oiled machine that had been years in the making. But what keeps it functioning with such precision is every individual who stands by and does nothing. Perhaps because they are either too comfortable, or content to sit on the fence, or too afraid to pick up the gauntlet in the fight against the evils of racism.

Only you can open your eyes and see what is going on around you.

Dad, along with thousands of West Indians and other non-white immigrants, played a pinnacle role in making Britain what it is today, in spite of the racism they faced. And this courage has been instilled in me. In 2020, I became the co-chair of the Race Equality Network at Waltham Forest Council, where I now work as a senior lawyer. I provide support and representation to non-white staff experiencing racism within the workplace. I meet with white directors and senior managers, and tell them *my story*, in the hope that they can gain a *real* understanding of how they can 'open their eyes' to bring about change. Dad's gift, his legacy to me, is no matter how many hills I have to climb, or bridges I will need to cross, I must never give up the belief I have... *in me*.

NOTES & ACKNOWLEDGEMENTS

I would like to thank my husband, Everton, for never complaining when all that could be heard was the tapping of a keyboard at 5 a.m every morning, and for providing words of encouragement when it all seemed like too much. My parents and sisters and brothers who have all been the foundation of my life, and who have allowed me to tell their stories, as well as my own. Finally, I would like to make an acknowledgement of those thousands of nameless enslaved people who died, fighting for my freedom.

1   Angelou, Maya. 'America's Renaissance Woman.'
    Academy of Achievement Interview, 22 January, 1997.
    [Online] https://achievement.org/achiever/maya-angelou/#interview
    [Accessed 7 June, 2021].

2   Powell, Enoch. Keynote presented to the annual Conference of the Rotary
    Club of London at the Burlington Hotel, Eastbourne, 16 November, 1968.
    [Online] https://www.enochpowell.net/fr-83.html
    [Accessed 16 September, 2020].

3   Devlin, Hannah. 'First Modern Britons had "Dark to Black Skin",
    Cheddar Man DNA Analysis Reveals', *Guardian*, 7 February, 2018.

4   Laozi (Lao Tzu). *Dao De Jing (Tao Te Ching)*, Chapter 64
    (literally translated as 'A thousand mile journey begins below the feet.')
    [Online] https://www.centertao.org/essays/tao-te-ching/carl/chapter-64/
    [Accessed 7 June, 2021].

5   'Notting Hill 58', *Time Shift*, BBC 4, first broadcast 10 August, 2005.
    [Online] https://www.youtube.com/watch?v=xeAaFlbRhRo
    [Accessed 7 June, 2021].

6   Davenport-Hines, Richard. 'National Service: Conscription in Britain
    1945–1963 by Richard Vinen – Review', *Guardian*, 20 August, 2014.

7   Warren, Tom. 'Is knife crime really increasing?'
    BBC News Channel, 11 July, 2008.
    [Online] http://news.bbc.co.uk/2/hi/uk_news/england/7502180.stm
    [Accessed 7 June, 2021].

8   Sword, Harry. 'Greased Quiffs and Switchblades:
    Growing up Teddy Boy in 1970s England', *Vice*, 2 February, 2015.

9   'Teddy Boys – 50s, TEDS, TV News Clip, HepCatmobile.
    [Online] https://www.youtube.com/watch?v=uBdbwnfRmsM
    [Accessed 7 June, 2021].

10 Blackman, Rick. *Forty Miles of Bad Road: The Stars Campaign for Interracial
    Friendship and the 1958 Notting Hill Riots*. London: Redwords, 2017, p. 19.

11 'Notting Hill 58', *Time Shift*, 2005.

12 'Notting Hill 58', *Time Shift*, 2005.

13 'Notting Hill 58', *Time Shift*, 2005.

14 'Notting Hill 58', *Time Shift*, 2005.

15 'Notting Hill 58', *Time Shift*, 2005.

16   Gildart, Keith and Howell, David (Eds.). *Dictionary of Labour Biography,
Vol. XIV*. London: Palgrave Macmillan, 1972, p. 215.

17   'Crimes of the century', UK Parliament Statistics, 2021.
[Online] https://www.parliament.uk/business/publications/research/
olympic-britain/crime-and-defence/crimes-of-the-century/
[Accessed 5 March, 2021].

18   Sherwood, Marika. *Claudia Jones: A Life in Exile*, London:
Lawrence & Wishart Ltd, 2000.

19   'Naomi Campbell on Racism in Fashion',
Channel 4 News, first broadcast 16 September, 2013.

20   'Hidden Herstories: Claudia Jones', *Our Heritage TV*, 10 July, 2018.
[Online] https://www.youtube.com/watch?v=HTT1nKQpTIk
[Accessed 13 February, 2020].

21   'Hidden Herstories: Claudia Jones', *Our Heritage TV*, 2018.

22   Blackman, Rick. *Forty Miles*, 2017, p. 20.

23   James, Winston. 'Migration, Racism and Identity:
The Caribbean Experience in Britain', *New Left Review*, 1/193 May–June, 1992.

24   'Martin Luther King – 1964'. *History Highlights*, St Paul's Cathedral website,
[Online] https://www.stpauls.co.uk/history-collections/history/history-
highlights/martin-luther-king [Accessed 5 May 2021].

25   Jeffries, Stuart. 'Britain's Most Racist Election:
The Story of Smethwick, 50 Years On', *Guardian*, 15 October, 2014.

26   Jeffries, Stuart. 'Britain's Most Racist Election, 2014.

27   Hansard 1964 UK Parliament

28   Wilson, Harold. Speech given at the Labour Party Conference,
Blackpool, 1965, UKPOL Political Speech Archive.
[Online] https://www.ukpol.co.uk/harold-wilson-1965-labour-party-
conference-speech/ [Accessed 16 September, 2020].

29   Larkham, Peter. 'Replanning London after the Second World War',
lecture given at Gresham College, 24 July, 2015, sponsored by The City of
London Corporation and the Mercers' Company.
[Online] https://www.gresham.ac.uk/lectures-and-events/replanning-
london-after-the-second-world-war [Accessed 7 June, 2021].

30   'Smethwick Council Buying Vacant Homes to Prevent More Coloured People
Moving in on Marshall Street', ITN Archive footage, 1964.

[Online] https://www.youtube.com/watch?v=yi-XGVc9wy4
[Accessed February 2020].

31 Bogdanor, Vernon. 'Roy Jenkins, Europe and the Civilised Society', Lecture given at Gresham College, 15 January, 2013. Sponsored by The City of London Corporation and the Mercers' Company.
[Online] https://www.gresham.ac.uk/lectures-and-events/roy-jenkins-europe-and-the-civilised-society [Accessed 7 June, 2021].

32 Collinson, Marc. 'Welsh History Month: Roy Jenkins, a more civilised society and Labour's "moral crusade"', Wales Online, 9 October, 2015 [Online] https://www.walesonline.co.uk/lifestyle/nostalgia/welsh-history-month-roy-jenkins-10227852 [Accessed 8 June 2021].

33 Bogdanor, Vernon. 'Enoch Powell and the Sovereignty of Parliament', Lecture given at Gresham College, 12 March, 2013. Sponsored by The City of London Corporation and the Mercers' Company. [Online] https://www.gresham.ac.uk/lectures-and-events/enoch-powell-and-the-sovereignty-of-parliament [Accessed 7 June, 2021].

34 Powell, Enoch. Keynote presented at the General Meeting of the West Midlands Area Conservative Political Centre, Birmingham, 20 April, 1968. (Now commonly referred to as his 'Rivers of Blood' speech.)
[Online] https://www.enochpowell.net/fr-79.html [Accessed 7 June, 2021].

35 Powell, Enoch, 'Rivers of Blood' speech, 1968.

36 Powell, Enoch, 'Rivers of Blood' speech, 1968.

37 Powell, Enoch, 'Rivers of Blood' speech, 1968.

38 Powell, Enoch, 'Rivers of Blood' speech, 1968.

39 Aitken, Ian. 'Enoch Powell Dismissed for "Racialist" Speech', Guardian, 22 April, 1968.

40 Jones, Nicholas. 'My Father and Enoch', Shropshire Star Weekend, 8 October, 2016. (Nicholas Jones was the son of Clem Jones, editor of the Express & Star, Wolverhampton from 1960–1970.)

41 Kabir, Nahid Afrose. Young British Muslims: Identity, Culture, Politics and the Media. Edinburgh: Edinburgh University Press, 2012.

42 Collins, Marcus. 'Immigration and Opinion Polls in Postwar Britain', Modern History Review, Vol. 18 No. 4, January 2016, pp. 8–13.

43 Crossman, Richard. 'Entry for 27 April 1968', The Diaries of a Cabinet Minister, Volume III. London: Hamish Hamilton, 1977, p. 30.

44 Hyde, John. 'Firm Advertises for Black Applicants to Fill Demographic Gap, *Law Gazette*, 18 September, 2019.

45 Hyde, John. 'Firm Advertises for Black Applicants, 2019.

46 'New CSI Report on Ethnic Minority Job Discrimination', Nuffield College, University of Oxford, 21 January 2019. https://www.nuffield.ox.ac.uk/news-events/news/new-csi-report-on-ethnic-minority-job-discrimination/ [Accessed 13 June 2021]

47 'Diversity at the Bar 2019', Bar Standards Board, January 2020. https://www.barstandardsboard.org.uk/uploads/assets/912f7278-48fc-46df-893503eb729598b8/28f8fbfa-3624-4402-9c8f83af837a1e60/Diversity-at-the-Bar-2019.pdf [Accessed 13 June 2021]

48 Powell, Enoch, 'Rivers of Blood' speech, 1968.

49 Powell, Enoch. *A Lexicon to Herodotus. pp. xii 392.* Cambridge University Press, The Classical Review, Vol. 52 No. 2, 1938, pp. 178–9.
[Online] doi:10.1017/S0009840X00074394 [Accessed March 2021].

50 Bogdanor, Vernon. 'Enoch Powell and the Sovereignty of Parliament', 2013.

51 Tomlinson, Sally. 'Enoch Powell: Empires, Immigrants and Education', *Race Ethnicity and Education*, Vol. 21 No.1, 2018, pp. 1–14.
[Online] DOI: 10.1080/13613324.2017.1365055 [Accessed 7 March, 2021].

52 In the August 24, 1957 issue of *National Review*, Buckley's editorial 'Why the South Must Prevail' spoke out explicitly in favour of temporary segregation in the South until 'long term equality could be achieved'.

53 Buckley, William F. 'Firing Line with William F. Buckley Jr.: The Trouble with Enoch', 19 May, 1969.
[Online] https://youtu.be/nN6sTBSAp-A, [Accessed March 2021].

54 Heffer, Simon. *Like the Roman: The Life of Enoch Powell.* London Orion Pub Co, 1999.

55 '1970 United Kingdom election', https://en.wikipedia.org/wiki/1970_United_Kingdom_general_election [Accessed 13 June 2021]

56 Travis, Alan. 'Ministers Saw Law's "Racism" as Defensible', *Guardian*, 1 January, 2002.

57 'Files reveal a dirty secret', *Manchester Evening News*, 21 August, 2007.

58 Abrahámová, Nátalie, 'Immigration Policy in Britain Since 1962', Masaryk University, 2007 . https://is.muni.cz/th/64569/ff_m/FinalDraft.pdf [Accessed 23 March 2021]

59 'Enoch Powell on Being Called A Racist', *The Dick Cavett Show*, May 1971 [Online] https://www.youtube.com/channel/UCFC8Vt3FY_7svm_SOBK5aIQ [Accessed March 2021].

60 Sriskandarajah, Dhananjayan and Drew, Catherine. 'Mapping the Scale and Nature of British Emigration', *IPPR*, 11 December, 2006.

61 'Brits Abroad', BBC World Overview, BBC News Channel. [Online] http://news.bbc.co.uk/1/shared/spl/hi/in_depth/brits_abroad/ html/default.stm [Accessed March 2021].

62 See: http://extranjeros.inclusion.gob.es/ficheros/estadisticas/operaciones/ con-certificado/202006/Residentes_Principales_Resultados_30062020.pdf [Accessed March 2021].

63 'BREXIT: How many Brits have left Spain and how many are staying?' *The Local*, 22 December 2020. [Online] https://www.thelocal.es/20201222/ brexit-how-many-brits-have-left-spain-and-how-many-are-staying/ [Accessed March 2021] (Also see footnote: 49).

64 The Race Relations Act 1976, *Sage Journal*, 1 April 1977, Notes and documents 405. [Online] https://journals.sagepub.com/doi/ abs/10.1177/030639687701800407?journalCode=racb, [Accessed May 2021].

65 *Hansard*, HC Vol, 906, cc1557, 4 March, 1976.

66 'Eric Clapton's Racist Rant', stillwerise.uk. [Online]: https://stillwerise.uk/2020/11/28/eric-claptons-racist-rant/ [Accessed 9 June, 2021].

67 Powell, Enoch, 'Rivers of Blood' speech, 1968.

68 'Who Shot the Sheriff?', written and directed by Alan Miles, film about the Rock Against Racism Movement 1976–1981 Mad Inertia 2005.

69 Silver Jubilee of Elizabeth II, Wikipedia. [Online]: https://en.wikipedia.org/ wiki/ Silver_Jubilee_of_Elizabeth_II [Accessed 11 July 2021]

70 Greater London Council Elections, Director General's Department of Greater London Council, Intelligence Division supplied by Returning Officers, 5 May 1977.

71 Bloom, Clive. *Violent London: 2000 Years of Riots, Rebels and Revolts*, London: Palgrave Macmillan, 2010.

72 Lewis, Ben and Klein, Richard (Directors). 'The Lost Race', BBC 2, first broadcast on 24 March, 1999. [Online] https://www.youtube.com/watch?v=SetkAwYSKtE

[Accessed 7 June, 2021].

73 'The Lost Race', BBC 2, 1999.

74 'The Lost Race', BBC 2, 1999.

75 'The British West Indies Regiment', Trench Brothers Education Zone website
    [Online] http://www.hmdt.org.uk/hmdtmusic/trenchbrothersteaching/6-
    the-british-west-indies-regiment/ [Accessed March 2021].

76 Trench Brothers Educational Zone website. The British West Indies
    Regiment. [Accessed 11 June 2021]

77 'The British West Indies Regiment', 2021.

78 'The Jamaica Prosecutions: Further Examinations of Colonel Nelson and
    Lieutenant Brand', *The Illustrated News: Law-Courts and Weekly Record*. London
    Vol. 1, 23 February 1867.

79 Winter, Sarah. 'On the Morant Bay Rebellion in Jamaica and the Governor
    Eyre-George William Gordon Controversy, 1865-70', *BRANCH: Britain,
    Representation and Nineteenth-Century History.* Ed. Dino Franco Felluga.
    Extension of Romanticism and Victorianism on the Net. Web.
    [Online] https://www.branchcollective.org/?ps_articles=sarah-winter-on-
    the-morant-bay-rebellion-in-jamaica-and-the-governor-eyre-george-
    william-gordon-controversy-1865-70 [Accessed March 2020].

80 Carlyle, Thomas. 'Occasional Discourse on the Negro Question',
    Fraser's Magazine for Town and Country, London, Vol. XL., February 1849.

81 Owen, Jonathan. 'British Empire: Students should be taught colonialism
    "not all good", say historians', *Independent*, 22 January, 2016.

82 In: Owen, Jonathan, 'British Empire:', 2016.

83 The Secret Teacher. 'Secret Teacher: the Emphasis on British History is
    Depriving Students of Balance', *Guardian*, 26 May, 2018.

84 Freeman, Colin. 'RIP Benny Green – The Boy Who Brought Black Britain to a
    Generation of School Kids', *Telegraph*, 25 May, 2015.

85 Hall, Stuart. 'It Ain't Half Racist, Mum', produced for BBC *Open Doors Series*
    in association with The Campaign Against Racism in the Media, Hosts Stuart
    Hall and Maggie Steed, March 1979. [Online] https://www.bcu.ac.uk/media/
    research/sir-lenny-henry-centre-for-media-diversity/representology-
    journal/articles/it-aint-half-racist-mum-transcript#

86 Hall, Stuart, 'It Ain't Half Racist Mum', 1979.

87 'The Lost Race', BBC 2, 1999.

88 'The Lost Race', BBC 2, 1999.

89 'The Lost Race', BBC 2, 1999.

90 'Has the American Dream been achieved at the expense of the American Negro?', James Baldwin debates William F. Buckley Jr, Cambridge University, 1965, Aeon video. [Online] https://www.youtube.com/watch?v=5Tek9h3a5wQ.[Accessed March 2021].

91 'James Baldwin speaks at UC Berkeley University', 1974, UC Berkeley, mobileaarmy. [Online] https://www.youtube.com/watch?v=8klsr2TB5pA [Accessed March 2021].

92 Coard, Bernard. *How the West Indian Child is Made Educationally Subnormal in the British School System*, London: New Beacon Books, 1971.

93 https://hansard.parliament.uk/Commons/1977-07-26/debates/d5bf9be3-084a-43b0-8e02-c2bcf4a28c81/WestIndianCommunity(Report) [Accessed 23 March 2021]

94 'West Indian Children in Our Schools Interim Report of the Committee of Inquiry into the Education of Children From Ethnic Minority Groups', *The Rampton Report*, 1981. [Online] http://www.educationengland.org.uk/documents/rampton/rampton1981.html [Accessed 7 June, 2021].

95 Vernon, Philip. 'Environmental Handicaps and Intellectual Development, Part I', The British Psychology Society, 1965.

96 'West Indian Children' (Rampton Report) House of Commons Debate, 6 July, 1981, Ellis, Tom MP, HC Deb Vol 8 pp. 237-44.

97 'West Indian Children', *The Rampton Report* 1981.

98 'West Indian Children *The Rampton Report*, 1981.

99 'West Indian Children *The Rampton Report*, 1981.

100 Education for All, Report of the Committee of Enquiry into the Education of Children from Ethnic Minority Groups', *The Swann Report*, 1985

101 Modood, Tariq and May, Stephen. 'Multiculturalism and Education in Britain an Internally Contested Debate', *International Journal of Educational Research* 35,vol. 35, p.305-317, 2001.

102 Beauvallet, Anne, 'Thatcherism and Education in England: A one-way Street?', University of Toulouse, November 2015.

103 The Marmot Review, run by the UCL Institute of Health Equity, who collaborate on works to address the social determinates of health and

improve equity. The Health Foundation, February 2020.

104 Grafton-Green, Patrick. 'Schools Accused of "Excluding Weak Pupils Before Exams" to Climb League Tables', *Evening Standard*, 28 August, 2018.

105 Grafton-Green, Patrick, 'Schools Accused', *Evening Standard*, 2018.

106 Demie, Feyisa. 'The experience of Black Caribbean pupils in school exclusion in England', *Educational Review*, Vol. 73, 2021, pp. 55–70.
[Online] DOI: 10.1080/00131911.2019.1590316 [Accessed March 2021].

107 'Education exclusion: How my son was unofficially excluded from school for 14 months', The Guardian. [Online] https://www.youtube.com/watch?v=1yr7dTdVHtE [Accessed 13 June 2021]

108 Truss, Liz. 'Fight for Fairness', GOV UK Speech delivered on delivered on 17 December, 2020.[Online] https://www.gov.uk/government/speeches/fight-for-fairness [Accessed 16 March, 2021].

109 Truss, Liz. 'Fight for Fairness', 2020.

110 Press Association. 'Student Ordered to Pay More Than £800 After 'Disgusting' Racist Chant', *Guardian*, 24 May, 2018.

111 Mitchell, Hannah. 'Sikh Student "Told to Leave Bar Because of his Turban" Said He Felt "Victimized" and "Discriminated"', *Nottinghamshire Live*, 10 March, 2018.

112 Long, Jonny, and Soen, Hayley. "'She's a big Ape': Boys insult BU Fresher in Racist Group Chat", *The Bournemouth Tab*, 14 November, 2017.

113 Thomas, Sophie. 'Racist Graffiti Written on Bananas in Warwick Halls', *The Warwick Tab*, 5 April, 2016.

114 Bouattia, Malia. 'Racist Incidents at Universities Show They Aren't as Tolerant as We Think', *Guardian*, 11 March, 2018.

115 'Actor Laurence Fox's Question Time Clash over Meghan Markle', *Question Time*, BBC One, first broadcast 16 January, 2020.

116 *Burning an llusion*, Shabazz, Menelik, Production Company, British Film Institute, released 1981.

117 '1981 Brixton Riots' : Wikipedia [Accessed March 2021.

118 '1981 Brixton Riots' : Wikipedia [Accessed March 2021.

119 'Enoch Powell: Civil Unrest, Racial Violence', *TV Eye*, Thames Television, first broadcast 16 April, 1981. [Online] https://www.youtube.com/watch?v=VTV1meyoSlM [Accessed 7 June, 2021].

120 'Enoch Powell: Civil Unrest, Racial Violence', Thames Television, 1981.

121 Scarman, George. *The Scarman Report: The Brixton Disorders 10-12 April 1981: Report of an Inquiry.* London: Penguin Books, 1982.

122 Scarman, George. *The Scarman Report.* 1982.:

123 Roberts Kenneth, Duggan, Jill, Noble, Maria, 'Unregistered Youth Unemployment and Outreach Careers Work: Final Report, Part Two', Outreach Careers Work. London, Department of Employment, Research Paper No. 32, 1981.

124 Scarman, George. *The Scarman Report.* 1982.

125 Scarman, George. *'The Scarman Report.* 1982.

126 Scarman, George. *'The Scarman Report.* 1982.

127 Scarman, George. *'The Scarman Report.* 1982.

128 Rose, David. *Climate of Fear: The Murder of PC Blakelock and the Case of the Tottenham Three.* London: Bloomsbury, 1992, p. 110.

129 Gifford, Anthony, *The Broadwater Farm Inquiry: Report of the Independent Inquiry into Disturbances of October 1985 at the Broadwater Farm Estate*, Tottenham, London: Karia Press, 1986, pp. 132, 144; Rose, David. *Climate of Fear*, 1992, pp.111–112.

130 Rose, David. 'Police Broke Rules in Hunt for Killers of PC Who Fell Victim to Bloodlust of the Mob', *Guardian*, 20 March, 1987.

131 Rose, David. *Climate of Fear.* 1992, pp. 50, 141, 145–6.

132 Rose, David. *Climate of Fear.* 1992, p. 152.

133 Rose, David. *Climate of Fear.* 1992, pp. 138–9.

134 Rose, David. *Climate of Fear.* 1992. pp. 21–4, 26–7, 91.

135 Bennetto, Jason. 'Silcott to be released from prison', *Independent*, 16 October, 2003.

136 McKillop, James. 'Second Life Sentence for Blakelock Killer', *The Glasgow Herald*, 20 March, 1987.

137 Rose, David. *Climate of Fear.* 1992.

138 Bennett, Will. 'Detectives "Fabricated Silcott Evidence": Notes Were Altered After Interview With Blakelock Murder Suspect, Court old', *Independent*, 29 June, 1994.

139 Rose, David. *Climate of Fear.* 1992, pp. 160–161.

140 Fennell, Philip W. H. 'Mentally Disordered Suspects in the Criminal Justice System', *Journal of Law and Society* Vol. 21, No.1, March 1994, pp. 57–71.

141 Guðjónsson, Gísli. *The Psychology of Interrogations and Confessions: A*

Handbook, London: John Wiley and Sons, 2003,

142   Rose, David. *Climate of Fear*. 1992, pp. 162–164.

143   Rose, David. *Climate of Fear*. 1992, pp. 169–170.

144   Rose, David. *Climate of Fear*. 1992, pp. 172–173.

145   Rose, David. *Climate of Fear*. 1992, pp. 172–173.

146   For 49 men and youths convicted, see: 'Britons vexed by election of cop killer', Associated Press, 2 May, 1989. For 359 arrested and 159 charged, not counting the six, see: Rose, David. *Climate of Fear*. 1992, p. 186, quoting Roy Amlot, (the prosecutor in the case).

147   Rose, David. 'Blakelock Jury Warned', *Guardian*, 20 January, 1987.

148   Barling, Kurt. 'Winston Silcott: Not Free Yet', BBC News, 27 February, 2004.

149   Taylor, Diane. 'Fall Guy', *Guardian*, 13 November, 2002; Taylor, Diane. 'Free at Last, But Still a Prisoner. Why Winston Silcott Refuses to Celebrate His Release After 17 Years Inside', *Independent*, 22 October, 2003.

150   Rose, David. *Climate of Fear*. 1992, p. 227.

151   'Obituary: Sir Derek Hodgson', *Daily Telegraph*, 21 October, 2002.

152   McKillop, James. 'Second Life Sentence for Blakelock Killer', *Glasgow Herald*, 20 March, 1987.

153   Rose, David. 'Three Get Life for Murder of PC Blakelock', *Guardian*, 20 March, 1987.

154   Rose, David. *Climate of Fear*. 1992, pp. 193–5.

155   Malik, Kenan. 'Creating the Beast of Broadwater Farm', *Pandaemonium* [Online] https://kenanmalik.com/2014/03/21/creating-the-beast-of-broadwater-farm/ [Accessed 7 June, 2021].

156   Rose, David. *In the name of the Law: The Collapse of Criminal Justice*. London: Vintage, 1996, pp. 300–1. For 'kickers and stabbers', see, Halliday, Josh. 'Keith Blakelock Murder Witness Denies "Fitting Up" Knife Suspect Nicky Jacobs', *Guardian*, 10 March, 2014.

157   Barrett, David. 'PC Keith Blakelock Murder Trial: Questions for Met Police as Nicky Jacobs Cleared', *Daily Telegraph*, 9 April 2014.

158   Bennett, Will. "Detectives 'Fabricated Silcott Evidence'",*Independent*, 1994

159   Bennett, Will. 'Detectives "Fabricated Silcott Evidence"', 1994.

160   Rose, David. *In the name of the law* 1996, p. 304; Bennett, Will. "Detectives cleared over Silcott case", *Independent*, 27 July, 1994.

161   Victor, Peter. 'Silcott officer will return in triumph',

Independent on Sunday, 31 July, 1994.

162 Rose, David. *In the name of the Law,* Vintage, *1996,* p. 304.

163 Travis, Alan. 'Oliver Letwin Blocked Help for Black Youth After 1985 Riots', *Guardian*, 30 December, 2015.

164 Travis, Alan. 'Oliver Letwin Blocked Help for Black Youth', *Guardian*, 2015.

165 Travis, Alan. 'Oliver Letwin Blocked Help for Black Youth', *Guardian* 2015.

166 Datham, Matt. '5 most shocking quotes in Oliver Letwin's "racist" memo', *Independent*, 30 December, 2015.

167 'Diane Abbot - Britain's first black female MP', The Barnet Group. [Online] https://thebarnetgroup.org/tbg/diane-abbott-britains-first-black-female-mp/ [Accessed 07 November, 2020].

168 Also see: The First Indian MP, Dadabhai Naoroji, Industrial & Imperial Migrations 1750-1900, [online] https://www.ourmigrationstory.org.uk/oms/dadabhai-naoroji-mp-for-central-finsbury-1892-1895 [Accessed 13 June 2021]

169 Schlesinger, P. and Tumber, H. *Reporting Crime: The Media Politics of Criminal Justice*. Oxford: Oxford University Press, 1994, p. 113.

170 Olins, Wolff. *A Force for Change: A Report on the Corporate Identity of the Metropolitan Police*, London, Wolff Olins Corporate Identity, 1988.

171 Olins, Wolff. *A Force for Change*, 1988.

172 Mawby, Rob. *Policing Images, Policing Communication and Legitimacy*, London: Routledge, 2002, pp. 28–36.

173 Hobbs, Dick. 'Lord Imbert: Metropolitan Police Commissioner Who Helped Modernise and Bring Public Scrutiny to the Force', *Independent*, 16 November, 2017.

174 Hobbs, Dick. 'Lord Imbert', *Independent*, 2017.

175 Rose, David. 'Right Attitude, Shame About the Leadership; Profile: Paul Condon 03 October 1998, *Independent*. https://www.independent.co.uk/life-style/right-attitude-shame-about-the-leadership-profile-paul-condon-1176148.html [Accessed 13 June 2021]

176 Mills, Heather and Ward. Stephen, 'Condon Resolute Over "Black Muggers", *Independent*, 11 July, 1995.

177 Buncombe, Andrew. 'Condon's Apology is Not Enough, Say Lawrences', *Independent*, 1 October, 1998.

178 'The Stephen Lawrence Inquiry: Report of an Inquiry by Sir William

MacPherson', Presented to Parliament by the Secretary of State for the Home Department by Command of Her Majesty, February 1999.

179 Cabinet Office National Statistics, revised December 2020.
[Online] https://www.gov.uk/government/statistics/civil-service-statistics-2020 [Accessed March 2021].

180 'Ethnicity Facts and Figures NHS Workforce', Gov.UK, 26 January, 2021.
[Online] https://www.ethnicity-facts-figures.service.gov.uk/workforce-and-business/workforce-diversity/nhs-workforce/latest
[Accessed March 2021].

181 'Ethnicity Facts and Figures, Judges and Non-Legal Members of the Judiciary', UK. Last updated 6 November, 2020.
[Online] https://assets.publishing.service.gov.uk/government/uploads/system/uploads/attachment_data/file/918529/diversity-of-the-judiciary-2020-statistics-web.pdf [Accessed March 2021].

182 Dodd, Vikram. 'Police "Too Slow to Change" After Stephen Lawrence Murder', *Guardian*, 18 April, 2018.

183 Jeffries, Stuart. 'Britain's Most Racist Election', 2014.

184 Powell, Enoch, 'Rivers of Blood' speech, 1968.

185 'Actor Laurence Fox's Question Time Clash over Meghan Markle', Question Time, BBC One, 2020.

186 Kebede, Rebekah, and James, Marlon. 'Why Black Women in a Predominately Black Culture Are Still Bleaching Their Skin', *Marie Claire*, 21 June, 2017.
[Online] https://www.marieclaire.com/beauty/a27678/skin-bleaching-epidemic-in-jamaica/ [Accessed 22 July, 2020].

187 'Global Skin Lighteners Market Insight 2020–2027: projected Impact of COVID-19, Businesswire'.[Online] researchandmarkets.com
[Accessed 22 July, 2020].